That Reminds Me

Linda Bartee Doyne

THAT REMINDS ME

DEDICATION

This book is dedicated to all my family and friends who have provided me so many memories of which I love being reminded.

ৈৈৈ

This book is written based on my own memories from my own brain's memory database. It is not my intent to be vindictive or to paint anyone in an unfavorable manner. In cases where I felt it best or did not have permission to use an actual person's name, I used an alias. If you recognize yourself in any of my stories, you will probably be the only person who will recognize you.

If my book offends anyone, please accept my apology.

If you like my book, that will make me happy and I thank you for taking the time to read it.

A Very Special Thank You
To
OUR TOWN BRENTWOOD
on Facebook
For the vintage photos of Brentwood, CA

To
Beverly, Carolyn and Lynn
For catching my typos and giving me feedback/

To
My Family
For not rolling their eyes every time I said:
"When I get this book finished…"

To
My Friends and Family
For encouraging me to write more, more, more…

Table of Contents

BEING BARTEE

We're a unique group – indeed, quite unique. We are a mixture of down-to-earth mixed with high-falootin' snobby; crazy and logical; blue collar, no collar and white collar; moral and just a tad off; generous yet close-fisted; trusting but guarded; and jovial even in the face of acute sadness. Yes, we are a breed unto our own.

When you are young you believe you are normal and that your family is normal, your life is normal, everything about you is normal. If you have lived nothing else, then of course, you believe your life is normal. I still believe that my family was basically normal. Oh, I know of some things that others might say were not so normal, but what do they know? Those outside observers have and do things I don't think is so normal.

My family was old-fashioned, Texas, Baptist who believed in the "Golden Rule" and that sparing the rod spoiled the child. If you were a child in Bartee World, you were raised by an entire family and not just your parents. "It takes a village to raise a child" would be appropriate for the Bartee's. Aunts and Uncles had almost as much authority over the children and the unspoken permission to discipline upon witnessing an indiscretion. They didn't "tattle" to our parents, they simply took action. That's the way things were done.

I remember that I, and my cousins, was often told to go get a twig from a tree to be used on our backsides. If you came back with a wimpy little twig you ran the risk of one of the uncles choosing one for you. Not a good idea. While I personally seldom had the effect of the twig on my body, I experienced it enough times to know that it was best not to disobey. We learned very early that the best course of action was to be respectful to our elders and be careful to be on your best behavior.

We had a patriarchy in our family. Men were dominate and in control. That is, until my Grandpa Gilson died and left my Grandma Nora in charge. She was a strong woman and although her three sons towered over her, she could make them do as she wished with a simple request followed by a certain "look." When Grandma set her mind to something, she got her way. She was respected by all and even at her gruffest, she was gentle and loving.

My mother was a rich city girl who fell in love with a dirt farmer. It was extremely hard for her to adjust to the new lifestyle that my father had thrust upon her. Grandma Nora and my Aunt Shirley were her ports in the storm. They became her mentors by teaching her things like how to kill a chicken, grow a garden, use a wringer washer and make a dinner that could expand the feeding capacity in an instant. My mother was a wonderful learner and in time it seemed she may have had the same Texas upbringing as my father.

All of the Bartee children were close. In fact, I once complained about not having any friends and my father quickly stated, "You don't need friends. You have cousins. You have family." They certainly didn't feel like cousins. They felt more like siblings. We were together almost constantly. As we grew up and moved on to our adult life, we were still close. We are a part of each other. We protected each other and fought with each other. We rescued each other and misbehaved together. It didn't matter how long we had been apart, when we saw each other again, the time apart seemed to fade away.

The Bartee clan was a group of jokesters. While we could be very serious and intense, we also could find a bit of humor in even the most disastrous of situations. Teasing and sarcasm was prevalent when the family got together – which was often. If you got mad because of the teasing, you would be told to toughen up. Growing a thick skin was a requirement for survival. If you didn't you would never get through a meal.

Ahhh… the dinner table… Every night without fail, everyone in the house gathered around the dinner table for our supper time meal. Mom called it dinner. Dad called it supper. Potato – Pataato. It wasn't a giant kitchen but somehow we often had up to 12 bodies at that table. We squeezed in, shared chairs, put a wide board over the back chairs and used it as a bench, squished in the red-seated step stool, and even had some dining at the counter. We could have moved into the large dining room, but it was way too formal for all of us. We just wanted to talk and eat.

Those dinner hours were some of the best of the day. We made plans, discussed problems, asked for permission, teased, joked, argued, cried and laughed. It was the one time when the family was completely together. Food was passed around the table starting at my father's end. Everything was served in big bowls with large spoons. It was customary to take a bit from every bowl even if you didn't like what was being served. You better eat what was in front of you because there would be no special orders and when the food was gone there would be no more until breakfast. We didn't have to ask for seconds, but my parents were watching. You must be sure to eat most everything before taking seconds. And, if it was the last of what was left of a dish, you must ask "Does anyone want any more of this?" If someone said they wanted more, the dish was shared between them. In any event, no one left the table hungry and we didn't have a lot of leftovers.

Being Bartee meant having a strong work ethic. The only holidays that were reasons for not working were July 4th, Thanksgiving and Christmas. Even then they often "checked on things", meaning that a barge must be kept from sinking or some such catastrophe prevented. As hard as we worked, we played and celebrated just as hard. On the rare occasion that time was taken off, we made every minute count. We had family camping trips, barbeques, and trips to visit distant family. We celebrated graduations, weddings, and even funerals. Work hard, play hard – that was the way to live a Bartee life.

Bartee girls were treated differently from boys. The boys had the responsibility of going to work with my Dad and helping him earn a living to support all of us. They learned how to drive piling, dredge a canal, take soil samples, pilot a tug boat while towing a barge. By the time they were in high school they could operate a crane, back-hoe and many other pieces of heavy machinery. They welded, repaired, fixed and invented. Being a Bartee boy meant you would always have skills to provide a means of making a living.

The girls learned the fine art of housekeeping. Girls learned how to keep a house spotlessly clean, do the laundry, including ironing everything except socks and underwear, plan and prepare meals, as well as tend to the babies. But the lessons did not stop there. Girls tended to the garden and learned to can and preserve the fruits and vegetables. We learned to do minor repairs because to wait for your man to do it may mean it never got done. We also learned to sew and repair clothing. By the time a Bartee girl graduated from high school, she would have all the knowledge she needed to be a superb wife, homemaker and mother.

A high value is placed on education. Because our aunts and uncles didn't have an opportunity to always finish high school or even think about college. There was a rule that all children finish high school. There would be no drop-outs in our family. When a high school diploma absolutely could not be accomplished, a GED was secured as soon as possible.

College was encouraged, but not mandatory. The boys were also encouraged, if not going to college, to work in the family business. Most of them did just that while a few managed to leave the construction world behind and make their own way. It was not expected but rather assumed that the girls would grow up, get married and have a bunch of kids. The assumption was often wrong.

The older generations of Bartee girls were not strangers to work. They not only worked the fields of the childhood farm, but stood shoulder to shoulder with their brothers in whatever they were doing. They didn't just grow up, get married and have babies. They were hair dressers, truck drivers, assembly line workers, short-order cooks. They contributed to the family household as a unit because they were a unit. They were individuals who were a part of a ONE. The family was everything. They lived together, played together, worked together, mourned together, and survived together. When the baby in the family of seven children, wanted to go to college and nursing school, the family pooled money to make the nursing school a reality. Together the entire family paid for whatever was necessary to help her achieve her nursing degree. She retired as a Commander in the Navy Nursing Corp.

Bartee's take care of our own. When a Bartee gets sick and cannot take care of his or her self, the family provides their own caretaking system. We seldom put a family member into a nursing home. Whether it be emotional or physical care, the family member attempts to provide what is needed. But, when one of us is in pain, no matter the generation, you will find a Bartee somewhere close by to provide comfort.

Not all of us share the same DNA. It was once said that being involved with a Bartee was like being in the Mafia. Once you're in, you're in for life. Unless something catastrophic has taken place, a person who wants to be in the family will be in for as long as they want. There have been occasions that a person has not remained a part of our clan, but usually it's by that person's choice.

Bartee's are adventurers. Our ancestry has been linked to Lewis Merriweather a famous explorer. Is it any wonder that we never feel lost? We may be temporarily disoriented, but never lost. However, the women never have a problem with asking for directions if it is absolutely necessary and time is of the essence. After all, it was

Sacawega who really set the course for Lewis and Clark. Being lost is just a way of seeing the countryside or other parts previously unknown.

Just like every other family, we have spats, disagreements, and periods where one faction may disown another. We even have had fist-a-cuff encounters when things get really heated. But, in the end, we somehow manage to find our way back to each other. There may be discourse within the unit, but if attacked by an outsider, we all stand firmly together. We are a force to be reckoned with.

Bartee's are patriotic. Sailors, Soldiers, Militiamen, and Rebels from every war – Revoluntary, 1812, Civil, World Wars, Koren War and VietNam and every war thereafter. We have been there. We have not just enlisted, we have fought. Our family contains many heroes and they have done so without much fanfare. We stand by America and the American way of life.

Of course, in a family this large, we have also been known to contain scoundrels. Some family members have been to prison and some have had difficulty adapting to the social norms of society. Those are ones who have been honestly dishonest and you would have to know their entire story to judge them. We Bartee's aren't keen on rushing to judgment on any person or situation. We know that there really are different shades of gray.

Life as a Bartee is never easy. But it is a life that, while as a youngster I did not like, as an adult I am appreciative of every single aspect. Different – YES. Easy – NO. Proud – without a doubt.

Nora Bartee, Alma and Elbert Davenport, Morris Bartee, Louisa Day Bartee and Gilson Bartee

Tom, Art, Nonnie, Beverly, Gilson, Lin, Richard and Steve

Shirley, Myrtle, Lois, Opal, Oletha, and Dot

THIS PAGE INTENTIONALLY LEFT BLANK.

You can write a story about your family dynamic, make notes, do some creative scribbling or play some tic tac toe.

INDEPENDENCE DAY

Independence Day, the day we celebrate our independence from Great Britain. It happens every year on the 4th day of July. Of course it isn't always celebrated on the 4th of July. In order to make sure everyone gets to celebrate, the actual day off is the Friday or Monday closest to the 4th of July. That gives workers a long weekend to enjoy time with family, a short trip, or just to be lazy.

I remember celebrating Independence Day with my family when we still owned property off Dutch Slough Road near Bethel Island. The entire family got together. People came from as far away as Cobb Mountain, San Leandro and Mill Valley. It is rumored that the count exceeded 60 attendees at any given count.

Several empty metal barrels were cut in half and a metal grates served as the grill top. Long tables were created using old doors resting atop saw horses. Giant sized washtubs were filled with ice covering the Nehi orange and grape sodas, Co-cola and beer. Gallon pitchers of sweet and unsweet tea were on a table next to the drink tubs.

There were enough hot dogs, hamburgers, ribs and steak to feed a small army. Everyone brought something; potato salad, deviled eggs, chocolate cake – if anyone went hungry is was because he or she was too lazy to go to the feast laid out on the table.

Food wasn't the only thing that created this awesome day. Softball games, horseshoes, bike riding, and endless conversations filled with laughter were just a few of the highlights. The older kids went skiing and some went fishing off the dock. This was family time at its best.

When I became a teenager, the family feast slowed down to include just a fraction of the former attendees. Our family had moved to Brentwood, the home of the Brentwood Lions Club Carnique. Lots of carni games were set out in booths along two sides of the town park. There were booths selling fresh corn on the cob, barbeque sandwiches and ice cream. A friend and I would walk around the park for hours, eat until we were stuffed, spend our money on the games, and come home with a bag of goldfish. If I was lucky, I'd win a candy dish or some other treasure that surely cost less than the money I spent trying to win it. I remember one year that my mother was a part of a synchronized swimming group that performed in the high school pool at the edge of the park. It was fun to watch her and the other swimmers work their perfectly timed routines.

The family always ended up back at my parents' house in time to watch the fireworks. We had a perfect view from our front yard. We spread out blankets and watched the light show without the annoyance of strangers crowding into our space. For me, this holiday was right up there with Christmas.

As I grew older and had children of my own, I hosted many 4th of July celebration cook-outs. When we lived in Virginia, we watched the fireworks being set off in Yorktown. Sometimes we would stroll the streets of Williamsburg on that special day in one of the most historical places I had ever been. On one occasion, we watched the fireworks from a friend's boat while moored in Hampton Roads just off downtown Norfolk. I believe those were the best fireworks, I had ever witnessed.

Independence Day now doesn't always include a big cookout or lots of family visitors. Mostly it is a quiet day that I spend reflecting on all those Independence Days gone by. I think about the word "independence" and relate it to events in my life. There was the day I gained independence from my parents when I turned 18; the day I divorced my husband; the days my children left home to start their own lives; the day I retired from my regular 9-5 job and renewed my writing interests; and, the day I realized that I could create my own independence while others were dependent on me.

Each and every Independence Day I give thanks for all the men and women who keep me from having this day taken away from all of us here in this country.

Every Independence Day is a good day.

Brentwood July Fourth tradition
Our Town Brentwood CA

BRENTWOOD PARK WAS A SEA OF PEOPLE FOR THE LIONS CLUB ANNUAL FOURTH OF JULY CARNIQUE Barbecued chicken, corn-on-the-cob, game booths and entertainment were capped off by fireworks display from football field

THIS PAGE INTENTIONALLY LEFT BLANK.

You can write your own Independence Day story, or just make a few notes or draw some stick figure fireworks.

DUCK HUNTING

My father and uncles were owners of a duck hunting "lodge" on Chipps Island across from Pittsburg. It was rustic, no flushing toilets, about 8 bedrooms with enough bunk beds to sleep six at a time, and a giant fireplace that you could walk right into when building the fire. Anyway, to me it always felt like some special bonding outing when the "guys" would go duck hunting. It seemed girls were not allowed.

The men would bring home lots of ducks and the women would pluck and clean and prepare them for the freezer. The whole family would get together and we would have a duck feed. The line was clearly drawn between the men and women.

I put up a fuss. I wanted to go with the men and bring back the ducks. I wanted to eat cold baloney sandwiches at the long picnic table in the cabin, drink hot chocolate and soak in the fireplace warmth.

Finally, my uncle came to my defense and said I could come. After all, my grandmother used to hunt with the men and was an excellent shot. And the very next time, I was off to the duck blinds.

We took the long tug boat ride in the wee hours of the morning across the Sacramento River to the Spoonbill Slough and then to the cabin. We then hiked out to the blinds. During the trip, I was advised and informed as to how things would go once we reached our destination. I said I understood and was ready.

My father and I were sitting in the blind. Some ducks were within range and my father stood up to take a shot. Ohhhhh... no... the realization hit me that he was going to kill those beautiful ducks. I was appalled! I had to think fast! I jumped up and from somewhere inside myself I heard a shrill noise. I burst into tears and cried that I didn't like duck hunting and wanted to go home.

All the men broke into laughter so hard they must have been wetting their pants. My brother was instructed to walk me back to the cabin. I stayed there until they were ready to go home. Each had a group of dead ducks with them.

I never asked to go hunting again and had no desire to ever shoot a gun or kill a living animal.

BETHEL ISLAND WINDS

The wind on Bethel Island sounds different to me than any other wind sounds I have ever experienced. It seemed the wind blew only through the tops of the trees and never really reached the ground. I've never read "Wind in the Willows", but I imagine that is exactly how it would sound. I loved it and on especially windy days, I would beg to spend the night with my grandmother because her house was surrounded by trees.

I could lie on Grandma's big bed and try to stay awake so that I didn't miss a single sound. In my mind I envisioned the wind to be strings of horizontal lines running through the air. The lines would have to bend and curve and would thread their way through the tree tops quickly. All this bending, threading and curving resulted in swooshing and wooshing and swishing noises that magnified as the lines were pushed harder when the speed increased. I wondered if there was some secret message being carried to my ears from some distant magical place. I always fell into a sound sleep before I could decipher the hidden meaning.

When the morning sunlight crept across the bed and covered my face, I would wake up and the sounds would be gone. I could smell the coffee and biscuits and knew that breakfast would be waiting. Grandma always made a big country breakfast and my other relatives would slowly amass around her giant wooden table. When they were all present they would fill their bellies in preparation for a hard day at work. The house was filled with chatter and laughter and serious talk. Plans were being made and schedules were being formed. But, for me... the adventure was over... at least for another few weeks when I would spend the night at Grandma's again and listen intently for the magical winds.

At my parents' house in Brentwood I discovered that if I sat outside with my back up against one of our many Apricot trees on a breezy day, I would almost hear a version of the melodic Bethel Island winds. My mother had given me an old black taffeta skirt which I used to form a tent-like structure over my head. In the darkness, I could close my eyes and just let my ears take over. I only concentrated on the sounds around me. All too often, the loudest sound I heard was that of my mother telling me to come inside before I caught a cold.

I believe that my effort to hear those comforting windy sounds was my first attempt at stepping outside myself and letting my mind take over. I cleared my mind of any other thoughts and just listened. I let my imagination form images of the sound waves, but it was not a forced vision. It was a sense of being totally free. If I could do that, I could "ride the waves of the melodic lines". I imagine some people take drugs to get that feeling so I can see why they could become addicted. But, I didn't need drugs because my mind was open without them.

As I grew older, I become more grounded with the here and now of everyday life. I had no time for such silliness as listening to the wind in the trees or trying to duplicate the sensation of riding the sound waves. I had school work and house work and duties as a big sister and other responsibilities. When I closed my eyes at night, my only goal was to fall sound asleep in order to be well rested.

The mother in me wanted to share the windy night sounds with my children. On stormy nights, I would turn off the lights and we would all climb into my bed and I would tell them if we were very quiet, we could ride the wind to magical places. They didn't have much patience for that and before long they were back in the living room watching some cartoon or sitcom on TV.

My life in the country as a senior citizen has enabled me to drift back into that state of peacefulness that lies within the lines of the wind noises. On special nights of thunderstorms and potential hurricanes, I find a strange calmness while others are panicking about taping windows and securing loose patio equipment. I do all the "proper" things, but in the end, I look forward to being in the dark and letting my mind go as it will. Of course, it's hard to keep my mind clear of thoughts of budgets, duties, and other mundane things. But, if I can keep it clear for a period of time, I find a much needed peace.

If only I could bottle that feeling and sprinkle it over the surface of the world... imagine what changes just might take place.

THIS PAGE INTENTIONALLY LEFT BLANK.

What sounds do you associate with a favorite place?

PEANUTS WALK

She was just a little girl. That is, she was tiny for her age. Her mother liked to say that she was petite, but the truth was, she was just a little girl. Everyone called her "Peanut" probably because she was always the smallest in the group. But, she was adventurous and curious. She had to be in order to not appear so frail.

It really wasn't a very long walk to school. Everyone she knew walked. It was common practice and it didn't seem cruel or unusual at all to walk the quarter of a mile. She wanted to do everything the other kids did, so she was happy when her mother finally told her she would walk all the way to school without her mother walking with her.

Peanut woke up early and carefully picked out just the right dress. She felt more grown up now that she got to walk by herself and this day deserved a special dress for the occasion. Yellow was her favorite color and her mother had just finished making her a yellow cotton dress with little flowers. That would be the dress. She pulled out yellow stockings and put on her newly polished oxford shoes. Her mother combed her hair into a single pony tail with two long curls hanging from the rubber band. She liked the way she looked.

Breakfast that morning was cooked cereal, toast and orange juice. It was her older brother's favorite breakfast and it was OK, but she'd rather have had bacon and eggs. It was always a race to tell Mom what they wanted first. The first one to tell her got what they wanted.

OK. Breakfast was done, teeth were brushed and she was ready to go.

Out the door she went into the cool but sunny morning. At the end of the driveway, Peanut turned right and walked right down the middle of her side of the road. Sycamore Avenue was a street that had Sycamore trees planted right down the middle. Cars can, and did, pass over from side to side of the road as they wished. Often it was to avoid the kids doing exactly what Peanut was doing – walking down the middle of one side of the road.

Peanut had gone the length of one house when she spotted something in the tree-lined median. It was shiny, so she went over to inspect it. Just a piece of tinsel and nothing she was really interested in keeping. She kept going by putting one little foot in front of the other. She saw her neighbor's children getting into their father's car. They waved and asked if she wanted a ride. "No, thank you," Peanut replied.

Highway Four was the main road through town and where Sycamore Avenue started. Peanut turned left and started to walk in the area under the trees that was farthest from the busy road.

Purple Thistles! They were *soooo* pretty, but when she tried to pick one, the thorn pricked her finger so she decided to keep walking.

But... wait... there... **over there...** was a patch of wild daisies. She raced over and picked one to put inside her book.

Now she could smell the melted solder from the welding shop. Her father had warned her to never look at the sparks of the welding machine. Peanut kept her eyes down and was careful to not look inside the shop for fear that she may go blind in the instant that she took a peak.

Just past the welding shop was the truck stop. Peanut knew to be careful because big, big trucks turned in and they probably couldn't see a person as little as she. Peanut slowly walked backwards so she would have a clear view of on-coming trucks.

Looking down she saw a shiny rock in a puddle. She stopped and squatted down to inspect the rock. Picking it out of the water mess would make her hands dirty so she decided to leave it behind. Her mind told her to keep walking. She didn't want to be late for school… but there was this can and it was perfect for her to kick out of her way. The can had mud on it and when the force of her foot met the metal, the mud splashed up onto her clean shoe. Darn! Now she'd have to clean it when she got to school.

School She HAD to get to school.

Mr. Cliff always stood in the door of the Chevrolet showroom and watched as the kids filed past on their way to school. He said "Good Morning!" and "Don't you kids dally now." When Peanut saw him she stopped and turned right at him to wish him a good morning

Griffith-Roberts Chevrolet

before he had a chance to greet her. "Peanut, you best be moving on, you're a little late."

OK. Peanut thought. I'll just keep walking but she would have to cross the street that was the entrance to the high school parking lot.

High school parking lot.

The teens drove fast onto the street and into the gate. Peanut feared they would not see her, so she waited and she saw absolutely NO cars coming – then scurried across as quickly as her little legs could take her.

This is where the road made a big curve. There were trees on one side and the fence of the parking lot on the other. She stayed close to the fence. Up ahead she saw what looked like a whole candy bar still in its wrapper.

She rushed over and stood perfectly still when she had the wrapper in her hand. But it was empty and now she didn't know what to do with the wrapper. She didn't want to throw it on the ground so she carried it with her holding it out a distance from her body. It was as though the wrapper had cooties and she didn't want to catch them. At the end of the fence was the entrance to the high school. She made a left and walked up to the front of the school in order to drop the wrapper into a trash can. Then she turned back around and headed back toward the street.

Her school was on the opposite of the street across from the parking lot. She could have crossed the street at the end of the fence, but there was no crossing guard. Peanut kept walking another block to the crossing guard.

"Good morning Peanut! Where's your mother this morning?"

"I'm old enough to walk by myself." Peanut stopped with her hands on her hips to give the indignant response.

"Well, you better hurry along because you're running a little late," said Miss Crossing Guard.

Peanut walked slowly by the Lion's Den so she could take in all  the smells of bacon, hamburgers and greasy French fries. This was where the high school kids came to get their lunch and she imagined eating there herself one day when she got to be in high school.

She made the left at the Lion's Den to walk on the sidewalk to the next crossing guard. A chain link fence lined one side of the walk. A stick was stuck in the fence, so she pulled it out and ran it along the fence, making a clanging noise as she past. But at the corner there was no crossing guard. There were no kids playing on the swings or jungle gym.

OH NO! thought Peanut. How can that be? I'm late! She ran across the street without as much as a glance for cars. Next she bounded up the steps and raced down the hallway as fast as could. She stopped at her classroom door and slowly peaked inside.

"Good Morning, Miss Peanut! So nice of you to join us today. Please take your seat."

Peanut thought back over her walk to try to figure out how she could be so late. She decided that tomorrow she would not pick any daisies because they were clearly to blame for her tardiness.

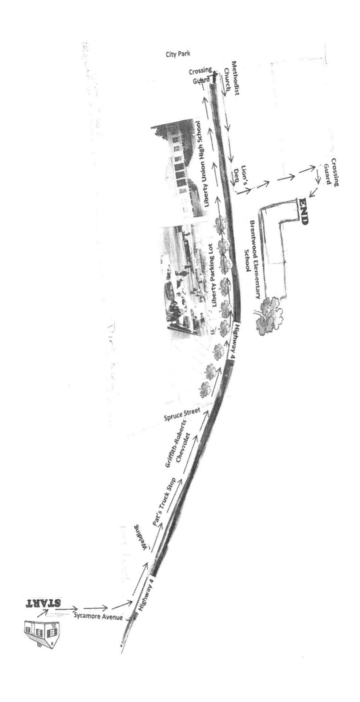

THIS PAGE INTENTIONALLY LEFT BLANK.

You can write your own story of getting to school, make notes or just do a little doodling.

DUKES UP

I remember being in the playground. A friend and I were walking around and watching all the other kids while we exchanged comments of fresh gossip. Somewhere from behind me a girl walked up to me and said "Irene is going to kick your butt after school today." I said, well… OK, but why? The girl responded with "You know why." Huhh?

I knew Irene and considered her to be one of my better friends. When she was sick I brought her flowers. We had sleep overs and went to the movies together. I couldn't think of any reason why she would be so angry with me.

I remember hearing the girl ask, "Where do you want to get the crap beat out of you?" The answer to that question seemed obvious. Instead of answering I just asked "Why doesn't Irene speak for herself?" At that, the girl ran off in the direction of the tether ball ring.

During lunch another girl came to my table, sat down and said "End of Spruce Street on the dirt road. After school today." The only word I could get out of my mouth was "Why". I had no idea what I had done that had provoked Irene's anger. I didn't start gossip and I made it a point to be nice to people – even ones I did not like. But I liked Irene.

I was not the bravest child and would go out of my way to avoid confrontation. I was small for my age and feared I was not as strong as the other kids. I didn't even know HOW to fight. On this day, I found my bravery. I walked over to Irene and said I did not want to fight with her. I said I had not done anything to hurt her and wasn't going to meet her at the end of Spruce Street or any other street. I told her to leave me alone.

"If you don't meet me, I'll go to your mother and tell her that you are threatening to beat me up. I'll tell the principal and I know they will believe me." So just let me clarify here – if I meet her on Spruce Street she's going to beat me up and I'll end up in trouble for fighting. If I don't let her beat me up I will be in trouble because she'll tell everyone that I was the one who wanted to fight. The dilemma of my situation was perfectly clear – there was no way to get out of this except to get it over with.

"OK. But there has to be some rules. No fists, only open slapping and we take turns." Irene and her crew were laughing at my suggestion, but Irene agreed. My stomach turned over when I knew I had just really dug a deeper hole for myself.

I arrived first at the designated "fighting" spot. I thought maybe she had changed her mind and wasn't going to show. But my thoughts quickly turned to fear when I saw her and about three other girls coming up the street. Spruce Street was a dead end that ended at a dirt road that ran crosswise from Spruce Street. It was often used by school kids as a short cut from Sycamore to Third Street.

Irene and I stood facing each other. She yelled "Take your best shot!" I tried. I really, really tried to raise my arm and slap her hard across the face. But, I just couldn't make myself do it. I barely tapped her. She laughed and then lunged at me. She was breaking the rules. I tried to push her off me but she was wrapped around me and wasn't letting go. Finally, I was able to get my hand under her chin and pushed her away. She fell backwards. I didn't wait for the next round – I ran home as fast as I could. I heard them screaming "Coward! Chicken!"

For the next five years, I avoided Irene as much as possible. It wasn't too hard to do. She hung out with a large group of girls while I preferred one or two close friends. I never found out why she was so angry with me. If I had known I would have apologized for hurting her.

I learned early on in life that I was not destined to be a person who ever won a physical confrontation. I lived in a house full of boys. They picked little fights with me all the time. But I managed to free myself and make it too much work for them to get to me. I learned to master the art of diplomacy and compromise. I was tiny and not so physically strong. A fight with me was like fighting a wet bath towel. Not much of a challenge there.

I talked it over with my BFF of the year and we agreed that no one won that fight. Certainly not me. And clearly not Irene. If she had wanted to have a fight with any meaning she would have chosen someone taller, stronger and more attuned to fighting. She picked a person who was clearly not her physical equal for no reason that I can determine. I'm not sure of her motive, but in my opinion she did not show any bravery in battling a weakling.

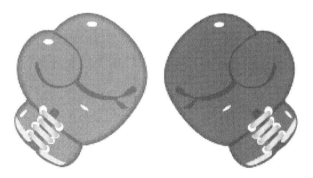

THIS PAGE INTENTIONALLY LEFT BLANK.

Did you ever have an encounter with a school mate that you would rather forget, but just stays there in your mind?

Write about your after school adventures in this space.

SUMMER JOBS

When I turned twelve years old, I was allowed to baby-sit for close friends and family. I went to my cousin's house every Saturday to watch after her two boys while she went grocery shopping. She lived in what I believe was called Garin Camp just off Walnut Blvd, between the railroad tracks and the road. It was a line of simple, low cost cottages. As time went on they had been revamped and added on to so that each was unique from the other.

My cousin's cottage had an extra bedroom off to the side and was the "boys" room. When I came to her house I cleaned starting with the kitchen and ending up in the boys room. By the time she returned from her shopping, her house was nicely clean. The two red-head boys (the only real red-heads in the family) were not difficult to watch after. They were well-behaved and never argued with me about anything.

In exchange for the day's work, my cousin would give me a shiny silver dollar and lunch from A&W Root Beer or sometimes from the Creamery. We would sit in her living room, look at movie star magazines and eat our lunch. Then she would take me home. I'm

sure many people would think that I worked too hard for the dollar. The only thing I can say is – well that's probably true. But it was a SILVER dollar and lunch was wonderful. Spending time with my cousin looking through magazines and talking girl talk was priceless.

I then ventured out to baby-sit for a couple that lived in the subdivision across the highway from us. They were a nice young couple with three small children. The couple would call on me to sit when they wanted to go to the movies. By the time I got to their house, the children were already bathed and ready for bed. All I had to do was sit and wait for them to return. I got paid fifty cents an hour and it was the easiest $1.50 - $2.00 I ever earned.

People started asking me to sit almost every weekend. It was my first experience with keeping a calendar and keeping track of my money. I also had to do some marketing to keep up the demand.

In August, I was asked to watch four children every day for two weeks. The father had to go out of town and the mother had accepted a work full-time. I had complete control over the four kids from 8 am to 4 pm. I made breakfast and lunch, cleaned house and played with the kids. Just before leaving, I would start dinner so that it would be prepared when the mother returned home. My parents took me to and from work and I gave the 50 cents a day for transportation. My pay was only 50 cents an hour, but it was $4.00 a day -- $40.00 for the entire two weeks. My cash stash was growing.

September came and I spent my entire bank on clothes and accessories for school. My parents bought everything that they considered to be "necessary" but I had to pay for anything not on that list. I bought a purse, shoes, some hair stuff. I loved having my own money to spend.

On my 14th birthday, I applied and received my work permit which would allow me to work at regular establishments, like Irene's clothing store. But, they only wanted to hire girls over the age of 16, so I did not qualify. Instead, a friend of mine told me she made good money by cutting apricots. She had worked for

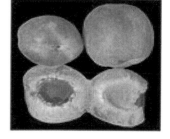

Wolfe Farms and suggested I apply. I filled out the application and started work with my friend as soon as the apricots were ready for cutting.

The process was to cut the apricot in half, remove the pit and place it on a large rectangular drying rack with the cut side up. The full trays were placed inside a drying oven and when the "cooking" was complete the result would be "dried apricots." The pay was per pound of pits. Each person had a "pit bucket" and at the end of the day the pits were weighed and recorded. There was no pay until the end of the season. I remember getting my very first ever pay check – and it was for more than $200! I remember thinking that I could buy a lot of stuff with that much money. I cut apricots for two summers in a row at the same place with the same people.

I learned valuable lessons from my working experiences. I learned to be reliable and to provide quality work. I learned to be respectful to the people in charge and to follow instructions. If I had lived in a larger town, I doubt I would have gotten employment as easily as I did. In a small town everyone knows each other and has an idea of who would be a good employee and who would not take it seriously.

I have immense gratitude for the Hamptons, Johnsons, Husteds, Martin and Wolfe families for giving me the chance to be dependable and help me utilize the excellent work ethic that was handed down by my ancestors. If you ever need a baby-sitter or apricot cutter, just remember I have experience!

THIS PAGE INTENTIONALLY LEFT BLANK.

You can write your own story and how you made money during the summer. Or just make notes, do some creative scribbling or play some tic tac toe.

CREDITS FOR MY FRIEND

Summers were hot in Brentwood. You could see the heat rise from the pavement. Air conditioning wasn't a standard in every home. Instead there were swamp coolers and fans. When it was hot it was hot. On the other hand, the nights were cool often requiring a light blanket for sleeping.

One particularly hot summer, my father moved our mattresses in the living room and dining room. The rooms were open to each other. At one end there were French doors and the other end had the big front door. If both doors were open we would get a nice cross breeze which cooled the entire area. Daddy opened all the doors and windows. We all slept soundly on those nights.

Grandma had come to live us and the heat made her so sick that we had to keep vigil over her. My uncles and father came up with an idea. They put two sprinklers on the roof and turned the water on. It was like a waterfall completely around the house. Within minutes the house cooled down. He left the sprinklers on until nightfall and turned them off. Our house must have been well insulated because the coolness held through until the next night.

There were solutions to the heat of the day for the kids. The most popular places to cool down were the swimming pool, library, and theater. If you ventured outside of town you might go to Orwood Resort or go skiing in Dutch Slough. Carrot and I would get our inner-tubes and float down river around Russo's Marina.

Going to the movies was something I could do easily because I was within walking distance to town. I could go to the afternoon movie and get a snack for under a half-dollar. I think it was twenty cents to get in, popcorn was twenty cents and a drink was ten cents. I could go with a friend or alone. It was one of the few things I was comfortable about doing by myself.

During intermission there would be a hula-hoop contest. I was pretty good at it and always joined in the competition. I was not athletic, but I could twirl that hoop around my tiny waist like nobody's business. Even if I didn't win that day, all hoopers received a free pass to the movies. I don't remember what you won if you were the best, but I was always excited to get the pass.

It was at the Delta Theatre that I really became friends with Doug. I had known him from grade school but we never became friends at school. After all, boys and girls didn't really become "friends" until the middle school years. Boys were icky and girls were all sissy. But, we knew each other. We knew who was who. We knew who would be mean and who would be nice. Being friendly at school was far different than being friends outside the classroom.

Somehow in the midst of the deep, dark, cool canyon that we called the Delta Theatre, Doug would see me and ask me to come sit with him. We shared popcorn and exchanged little remarks about the movie plot or the quality of the actors acting. Even in serious movies Doug would have me laughing so hard that a flashlight would end up being flashed in our faces. When the movie was scary, I would hide my face against Doug's should while pulling his shirt to my eyes so I wouldn't see the gory stuff. He always laughed at me and told me when it was safe to look.

When we became a few years older we would hold hands for a while and once or twice there were some kisses exchanged. But, it was never like boyfriend-girlfriend stuff. It was like… oh, OK, that was nice, oh, did you see that! He shot that guy! Doug and I were movie buddies. Sometimes I would confide in him and he would listen. Instead of giving me advise he would come up with some kind of cut-up response that made me laugh.

Doug and I nodded to each other as we passed in the high school hallways. We were polite, cordial and knew we were still friends even if all we shared was the quick "Hi! Nice to see you!" conversations. He seemed to have girls around him all the time. I perceived him to be something of a Casanova playboy. He was also a jokester, he could probably be voted as the person most likely to get into mischief. In spite of all that, I knew if I ever needed to I could simply call him and he would be there.

Sometime around 1974 or 1975, I had returned to Brentwood while my husband was on deployment in the Mediterranean Sea. I had run into a few high school friends during trips to the grocery store or other errands. People knew I was back. I don't know who told Doug that I was back, maybe one of my brothers or cousins, but he called me one evening.

To tell you the truth, I don't remember very much about the details of the conversation. What I remember most about the conversation was him asking me questions about my marriage, my kids, my life. He asked me to have dinner with him. Through it all he was teasing and playing around. At first I thought he was joking about dinner but somewhere, somehow, I realized that he really wanted to take me to dinner. I protested that I was married and it would in inappropriate for me to go on a date with another man while my husband was at sea. I was seeing his request as the prelude to something romantic and that could not happen.

In the early 70s I was not as enlightened as I became over the years. In the 80s I would have accepted the invitation without hesitation. I had come to realize that men and women actually could spend time with each other without a romantic overtone. I would not have worried about what "other people" thought. I would not have worried that it might upset my spouse. I would have happily accepted Doug's invitation and looked forward for our dinner.

Now, as all the memories from my past keep floating to the surface, I think about Doug my movie buddy. I remember the dinner invitation. The thought of finding him and asking him what he thinks of the movie I just saw is in the forefront of my brain. I'll never know because Doug died in 1986 and I'm just finding out in 2015. How sad is that?

With the exception of a few, I don't live my life regretting all my bad decisions. I prefer to think of them as learning lessons. However, I do regret that I said no to Doug. I regret that I didn't repay the friendship he had always shown me, by doing that one simple thing for him. I regret that I was not in California at the time of his death and could not go to his memorial service even if I had known that he died. Isn't it strange that I had not even thought about him until this weekend and now, I miss him.

When my life is at an end and the credits scroll up, Doug will be listed in those credits.

Douglas E. Hendrix (1948-1986)

Movie Buddy and Friend

THIS PAGE INTENTIONALLY LEFT BLANK.

Here you can make notes of the movies you enjoyed most as a child. Maybe you would like to draw a picture that represents your movie favorites. Did you have a special friend that enjoyed going with you to the local theatre?

BOOKWORM

Another way to spend those long hot summers in Brentwood was simply to find an air conditioned place and spend as much time as you can in that cool spot. One of those places for me was the Brentwood Library at 617 Second Street.

The library was a converted house that was right next door to what used to be the Masonic Hall. I remember it being goldish yellow

Old Brentwood Library

with lots of trees in the tiny front yard. There was a little porch with a screen door that would slam shut if you did not catch it in time. I believe the building is now used by the Brentwood Women's Club.

As you entered through the front door, Mrs. Tennant's desk was on the left. She always had carts of books around her. Her glasses hung around her neck on a pearlish beaded chain. Her hair was a reddish color and soft waves framed her face. I thought she was beautiful. I had seen her at our church many times and I knew her children. They were close to my age and we were often in activities together.

One summer afternoon, I walked from my house to the library and checked out a couple of books. I took my time looking around the shelves and checking to see the new arrivals. I decided on the first two books in the Laura Ingalls series.

Mrs. Tennant explained that I had two weeks to return the books before I would be charged a fine. I understood. She then asked how my parents were and if I had any plans for the summer. I told her my parents were fine and that I'd probably be going to visit my two cousins at each of their homes for a week. I further explained that one lived in the mountains and the other in the city. With the check-out process completed, I grabbed my books and bounced out the door and down the library steps.

At the end of 4th Street, there was a dirt road that would take me directly behind the high school and all the way to Highway Four at Sycamore Avenue. Before the apricot orchard across the street from our house was torn out to make room for tomatoes and lettuce crops, I could go from the dirt road at the end of Spruce Street straight through to my driveway. It was shady which provided some relief from the scalding sun. This was the shortest route from my house to the library or anywhere else downtown.

When I turned onto the dirt road, I opened up the first of the books. I walked slowly while reading and glanced up to make sure I was still on my dedicated route and not stumbling into ditches or ruts. By the time I got home, I had read several chapters. I was engrossed in the book by this time.

I sat in my room next to the open windows. The fan created a gentle breeze that kept me reasonably cool. As I read, I became a part of the book. I imagined myself as Laura and whatever was happening to her was happening to me. When my mother called me, it was like a vacuum was sucking me back into reality. I could feel my body as being paper thin and folding almost in half and winds surrounding me, pulling me up off the floor and into a different dimension. I resented each time I was brought back into the here and now and hurried to get back to the prairie as Laura.

Two days later, after finishing both books, I was back at the library. I checked out three books this time. Before long, I had read all the books in the series. By the middle of August I had read almost every book in the young adult section. I was in the library every other day, searching for something more to read.

Mrs. Tennant called my mother and asked if it would be OK if she suggested some books in the adult reading section. My mother knew Mrs. Tennant would not allow me to check out an inappropriate book so she consented. Now when I would come into the library, there would be two books waiting for me.

School came back into session the first week of September and the Friday before, I returned all my books back to the library. I knew that I'd not be spending much time there when school was in session. I would have homework and chores so there wouldn't be much time for casual reading.

I was saved by the fact that each week we had a library hour in the school library. I checked out a book each week and managed to escape to whatever imaginary world the selection would allow. Although now I also knew the library was a wealth of information on other topics. I read about etiquette and drawing. I did research for class projects. If I ever wanted to know anything, I knew I could find it there.

I'm thankful that I could escape the hot summer days simply by going to a place where it was cool and welcoming. I'm thankful that Mrs. Tennant encouraged me to read anything and everything.

Reading is something I do even to this very day. I don't have as much time for it as I used to and I can't keep up with all the authors' names and genres. But, when someone suggests a book for me to read, I do the best I can to really escape into it. It's the very best escape from reality without the use of drugs.

THIS PAGE INTENTIONALLY LEFT BLANK.

You can write your own story on how you escaped the heat of
the summer or how you spend your summer vacations..

THIS PAGE INTENTIONALLY LEFT BLANK.

You can write your own story of how you spend your summer school break, make notes or draw funny pictures..

INFORMED CHOICES

Sometimes my mother would go days without a car in her driveway. It was a bother to her because she couldn't transport her kids to places they wanted to go, pick up few things at the grocery store, etc. But, it was OK because she had children old enough to walk to the store since town was close by. My older brother and I didn't mind the hike because Mom always gave us enough money to stop for a treat on the way home.

LIONS DEN

Brentwood

Our Town Brentwood CA

The Lion's Den was between our house and the store so it made the perfect pit stop. A popular meeting place for teenagers, they specialized in burgers, fries and milkshakes. I never knew what Richard would order, but for me it was always an ice cream cone. He always knew exactly what he wanted the minute we arrived at the sliding window. Me – well – not so much. I knew I wanted an ice cream cone, but the issue was what flavor I wanted to order. I knew the menu front and backwards. But, what if they had changed something since the last time I was there? What if they added or deleted certain flavors? How would I know if I didn't ask?

One day we arrived at our place of special treats and, as I enjoyed the smell of grilling hamburgers and greasy fries, Richard ordered a larger order of fries and a Root Beer with just a little ice. The lady inside called out the order to the cook and then turned her gaze on me. Oh, it was my turn but I wasn't ready yet.

I thought about all the things they offered. I knew when Richard's fries arrived; I would want him to share a couple. Did that mean I should order something that could be shared? If I didn't order onion rings or a burger, would he not share his fries with his little sister? I knew I wanted ice cream and I didn't want his slobbery old tongue taking a lick from my cone. The lady in the window shifted her stance and said, "Do you want to order?" Well, of course I wanted to order. I just didn't know what to order. Richard gave me a "look" and I knew I better step it up.

"What flavors of ice cream do you have?" I asked the nice lady. She responded with "Chocolate, Strawberry, Vanilla, Rocky Road and Orange Sherbet." Then she waited for me to choose. Quickly I announced I would have an Orange Sherbet Cone, double scoop please.

Our food appeared in the window and Richard handed the money over plus a little tip. As we walked away he offered me some fries. Oh yes, thank you.

"We stop here all the time. You always order the same thing. But, you always ask what flavors they have. Why do you do that? You know what flavors they have. Richard seemed confused by my method of decision-making.

"Something might have changed since we were here last time. I thought maybe they might have gotten a new flavor." I responded.

"Why not just ask for the flavor you were hoping they would add?" he asked.

"I might not know I want a different flavor until I hear her say the name – like Butter Pecan. Maybe I didn't know I wanted Butter Pecan until she said it." It all seemed very logical to me.

"If you know you want Butter Pecan you should just ask for it. They'll tell you if they don't have it." Richard thought he had the final word.

"I just like to know all my options." We finished the walk home in silence.

THIS PAGE INTENTIONALLY LEFT BLANK.

You get it by now… write your own story, make notes, do some creative scribbling or play some tic tac toe.

RAINBOW

The International Order of Rainbow for Girls is an organization for young girls between the ages of 11 through 20. The Masonic affiliated service-based organization teaches skills in leadership, confidence and citizenship.

I watched my cousin in her formal gowns going to the Masonic Hall to be among her Rainbow Girl sisters. I was so very envious of her. During her installation as Worthy Advisor (the equivalent of holding the office of president), she had white and red colors for her theme of "Love." She had Bibles carved from Styrofoam with red ribbons and white and red flowers. I think it was the first time I had gone to a Rainbow event.

The young ladies swirled around in their gowns like southern belles. The hoop skirts gave the layers of lace, tulle, satin and taffeta skirts volume which made their waists look even tinier than they were. They were beautiful. Each and every one of those girls looked incredibly refined, composed, confident and classic. I longed to be one of them.

When I finally reached the age where I could join, I pleaded with my parents to allow me to become a member. My parents were both Eastern Star and Masonic members. In fact, I came from a long line of Masons. It didn't take much convincing for them to sign the application papers.

I had many friends who were already involved in Rainbow and I was very happy to join them. This is where I really felt that I belonged. It didn't matter what circle you associated with in school or how many "popular" friends you had, inside the Rainbow

Assembly, we were all sisters. I never felt excluded or uncomfortable. Any and all activities were places where I was always welcome.

We had slumber parties and no one ever slumbered until it was almost time to go home. It was one of my favorite social activities. But, Rainbow is a service organization and we held rummage sales, car washes and pancake breakfasts with the money being donated to a charitable cause. We supported the Masons and Eastern Star by serving at pancake breakfasts and other functions. Each year we participated in a competition at the county fair – usually a landscaping challenge.

Holding an office in Rainbow meant you must learn to speak to a group of people with confidence and clarity. The processions meant learning how to walk with grace rather than being the awkwardly clumsy person I naturally was. Although most of us already had a keen sense of respect for our elders, we learned to appreciate what the older generation could teach us. We were expected to hold ourselves to certain values such as integrity.

I was not a beautiful teenager. I had buck teeth and wore braces until the end of tenth grade. My hair had a mind of it's own. I stumbled over my own two feet and often got tongue-tied if anyone spoke to me. But, wearing that evening gown with my hair all done up and wearing high-heel shoes, I felt like I was one of the most beautiful girls in the room.

Before I joined Rainbow, I was a shy little girl who was afraid of her own shadow. I would not stand up for myself and I would not speak up. By the time I left Rainbow, I could openly hold a conversation with anyone around. I was not shy about expressing my opinions and sometimes that did not play well in my favor. I was not bothered if I had to give a speech or an oral report. I also learned diplomacy and tact. And I learned that although I was not a part of the cliques at school, I was not inferior. I knew why I wasn't in a clique and it really had nothing to do with anything except my own comfort level. That comfort level grew from being in Rainbow.

Rainbow did not make me a perfect person. We all have to learn from our mistakes and after leaving home, I made my fair share. From having been in Rainbow, I knew and maintained that I could make things happen to better my life if I strived to be the best person I could be.

I've always said I would not repeat my high school years for any amount of money. The only exception would be my Rainbow experience. If I could, I'd go back and do it all over again and again and again.

Isn't it ironic that my favorite station (position) was Immortality and I end up with a blog based on immortality? The color of that station was green and one of my favorite colors is green. Sometimes, some things are just meant to be.

Beautiful girls in beautiful gowns.

THIS PAGE INTENTIONALLY LEFT BLANK.

STOLEN OPPORTUNITY

Every day I passed by that big temple-like building with the words Liberty Union High School etched across its face. Inside there were real hardwood floors and paneling. The handrails above the few

steps were real wood. The doors to the office and classrooms were heavy and dark — more real wood. Years of patina had set in giving them a certain shine without the aid of a good waxing. When walking into the building through the big, glass-paned doors from the outside, you knew you were in a place of history. It almost felt sacred.

Front of Liberty Union High School before the fire.

Through my entire eight grade school years, I passed by the stately building. The high school was directly across the street from the grade school and in my direct route to the middle school. On rainy days, I would take a short cut through the covered walkways from one side to the other providing me a dry route for a short distance. I loved it inside the corridors, but I knew I did not belong there and made my way as quickly as I could in hopes that I would not be noticed.

On warm days, teenagers adorned the front of the old school. They sat on the steps and ledges, talking, laughing, gossiping, and/or posing. Sometimes a few of the girls would help a grade-schooler cross the busy highway that ran between the two schools which saved an extra block of walking to the crossing guard. Occasionally, the mean kids would be out and would yell derogatory comments at the children. But, the other teens quickly countered the mean ones with words of encouragement.

As a child, I saw those teenagers as being what I longed to be — a person who has attained the age range of 14-18. Those were supposed to be the years that would give me freedom and privilege. It was when my parents would stop telling me I wasn't old enough to do whatever it was I wanted to do. It was a time when I could make my own choices. I could not imagine life after four years spent in that school. I had no concept of high school leading to something else. I knew I would go to college — but that was so far off and there was no "tangible" for the idea. This building that housed the high school was something I had seen my entire life — it was real and it was now. And it was bigger than anything I had ever known in the past.

As of September 4th, 1962, I actually belonged inside those walls. This was now MY school and I felt as though I had joined an elite group of individuals. My presence here would now and forever be joined with thousands of other students from so many previous years who were all a part of the history of this place.

You could smell the leather and wood when you walked into the library hall. Many of my relatives had wandered the aisles between the shelves searching for reference material. They passed notes in study hall and spent detention time in this very room. The library was my favorite place in the entire school.

On March 24, 1963 a fire was started in that very library that I had so coveted. Arsonists, rumored to be a group of disgruntled students, had destroyed a large portion of our high school. My beloved library was gone along with all the sights and smells that it had possessed.

Several days after the fire, I stood in front of the charred stucco building just the same as many others had during those days. I couldn't help but cry. My tears were for the loss of the opportunity to spend time in those same rooms as my relatives had before me.

Demolition to make way for new construction.

The town joined with school officials to get classes started once again. They farmed us out to the Veterans Hall and Methodist Church. The girls' gym was divided into classrooms. Learning was difficult in those noisy, chaotic rooms. As hard as the school administrators tried — there was no sense of normalcy in our regular school day.

When school opened in my senior year, we entered a new school building and I got the privilege of experiencing the smells of fresh paint and new carpet. The buildings were modern and efficient. But they did not hold the character or charm of the old buildings. There was no hardwood flooring or paneling — no smells of aged leather or wood. The class of 1966 experienced just a bit of the past and a bit of the future and in between we just "made do" with whatever was handed to us. We were the first graduating class of a new era at Liberty Union High School.

Since then, my little brothers, nieces and nephews have been able to do what was snatched away from me — they can sit in the same chairs, learn the same lessons and be within the same four walls as previous family members. But it's different now. Instead of hallowed halls, the school is now simply an institution of learning devoid of much personality. I don't know if losing these new buildings would be as traumatic to them in 2012 as it was for us in 1963. Somehow, I doubt it. And for them I feel sad for their loss of the opportunity to experience how things were before the Liberty fire of March 24, 1963.

A New Liberty Union High School -- 1965

THIS PAGE INTENTIONALLY LEFT BLANK.

You can write your own story, make notes, do some creative scribbling or play some tic tac toe.

THIS PAGE INTENTIONALLY LEFT BLANK.

Mustang Nightmare

It was September 1965 and school had just begun. The days were still warm and the evenings were cool. There was still a slow and easy pace about town. My father needed to pick up a part for some piece of equipment or something and asked if I'd like to ride along. The trip would take about an hour each way. Sure, I'd love to have some one-on-one time with him.

On the same day, my mother needed to get a part for her washing machine. She had been up all night with my youngest brother. My oldest brother, Richard, had left his brand new Mustang for her to drive to the parts house. As much as she needed the washing machine to be fixed, she was just too tired to drive.

My cousin, Steve, was staying with us for his last year of high school. He volunteered to run the errand for my mother. Not knowing how Richard would feel about someone else driving the Mustang, Mom was hesitant. She knew that Richard was very particular about who drove his car.

Steve reassured my mother that it would be a straight shot there and back. In fact, my two younger brothers could ride with him if it made her feel better. The younger, grade school age boys would make it more difficult for my cousin to run amok so she relented.

My father and I had just returned home when a highway patrol car pulled in to our driveway. The boys had been in an accident and were being transported to the hospital. My mother was crying. Daddy's big hand was wiping his face in a downward motion from forehead to chin. The baby was crying. I stood there like a zombie. My handed Terry to me and I bounced him up and down trying to get him to stop crying. My parents said nothing to me. They got in the car and drove off. I surmised they were going to the hospital.

The living room seemed like a vast open room without any hiding places. I didn't know when the baby had gotten his last bottle or his last dose of Tylenol. I focused on him. Change the diaper. Give him a bottle. Put a dropper of Tylenol in his mouth. Rock him gently. He calmed down and fell asleep.

Richard and my other cousins had been working all day. They would be hungry when they got home. I started preparing dinner. I did not cry. I was not sad. I was scared because I had no idea of what was going on. But, dinner needed to be fixed. People would be hungry and it was up to me to feed them.

I was just about done with dinner when my older cousin walked through the door with her two little boys. I asked her if she knew anything and she told me "Not yet." The rest of the guys filed in and we gave them the news. They ate and left for the hospital.

My boyfriend, Bobby called. I finally started crying. I knew nothing. No one had told me anything. Could he come over? Yes. He'd be right there. I turned the baby over to my older cousin, Nonnie, and Bobby and I headed to the hospital. My father pulled me aside in the waiting room.

"Both boys look very bad. Bruce looks the worst, but really it's Gary that is most in trouble. It will be shocking to see them, but you can't show that. Your mother needs to you to be calm and not upset. She can't help you now. She has to focus on the boys." I promised I would not upset my mother and was allowed into the room.

They were so fragile. So pale. Bruce had a cast from his waist to the big toe of his left leg. The leg was raised by a pulley. He had bags of fluid running to his arms and a mask over his face. Almost his entire face was bandaged. He looked like a sleeping mummy.

I turned my attention to Gary, who as a newborn was so tiny that he slept in my doll's bed. He seemed tiny again. He was tightly tucked in all around his body with his arms on top of the covers. There was a large hose somehow attached to his nose. A machine was pumping air into his lungs. Identical bags of fluid were being given to him.

Both boys were cut and mangled over every exposed piece of flesh. I could not imagine what pain they must have been in. I wanted to faint, but Bobby held me up.

The boys were not expected to make it through the night. Relatives were being called from all over the country and were flying in from various airports. No one wanted to leave the hospital so Bobby volunteered to be our taxi driver.

My mother had me pack her a bag so she could stay at the motel next to the hospital. My aunt flew in from Florida to be with my parents. I was told that I needed to take care of the house and Terry. I knew what that meant and I reassured them that I would do my best to make sure things were OK at home.

In the days and weeks that followed I had things I had to do. I accompanied the insurance adjuster to view the totalled Mustang. It still had pieces of Bruce's scalp hanging onto the jagged edges of the glass spears that used to be the windshield. The gear shifter was twisted and resting in the passenger seat. The front passenger seat back was sitting sideways across the seat. The steering wheel was hanging loosely from the column. The white interior was marred with streaks of my brothers' blood. My stomach turned and I vomited before I got back into the adjusters car.

My father had his own problems adjusting to the near loss of his male off-spring. He handed me a brown grocery bag and told me I had to wash the contents. I didn't think much about it and placed it on top of the washer. Days later, I looked inside the bag and found the clothes that had been cut from the boys bodies. They were hard where the blood had dried into the folds. Bits of glass fell from them as I held them up. There was nothing left except shreds of cloth that once was a shirt or a pair of pants. My aunt was with me that day and told me to put everything back in the bag and burn it. She told me to never mention it to him and he would forget. As I lit the fire I prayed, "Please, God, give me the strength to lie to my father if he asks about these clothes." I watched as the flames cleansed the evil from the bag. My aunt was right because my father never asked about the clothing.

I developed a routine: Up at 5am to fix breakfast for everyone before they left for work; Get Terry ready for Nonnie to pick him up; Get ready and go to school; Nonnie picks me up after school and brings Terry and I home; Clean up around the house; Give Terry a bottle; Prepare dinner; Clean up the dinner mess; Do some homework while Daddy gives Terry a bath and gets him ready for bed; Rock Terry to sleep with his bedtime bottle; Lay out my clothes; Get some sleep and start over the next day.

I finally found out what had happened during that trip to get the washing machine part. Steve fell asleep and ran a stop sign ramming head on with an oncoming car. The other driver was killed instantly. Bruce was in the center of the back seat. He was thrown forward between the front seats, hitting his left leg while breaking off the gear shifter, then through the windshield tearing off the skin on his face down to the skull, and then back through the windshield further removing the skin, and, again catching his leg on the gear shifter. He had multiple compound fractures of his left tibia. His facial skin and scalp had to be grafted back onto his head. Although his injuries were mostly external, it would take years of physical therapy and plastic surgery for him to ever have a normal life again. He would not be home any time soon.

Gary was thrown from the car and his body dragged along the road. He had massive head injuries, damage to his eyes, and internal bleeding. Although his injuries were more life threatening than his brother's, if he recovered from the first few days, he would recover completely in a much shorter time than Bruce. He would be home in about six weeks.

After a bit more than month, Gary was released and came home. His eyesight was damaged and he would need to wear glasses. But that was the extent of his injuries. My mother moved back home with him and we fell into a routine that almost felt normal.

Bruce was in the hospital for almost a whole school year. His leg was in traction and he needed extensive plastic surgery for the deep scaring of the skin that had been pulled back up over his face and skull. He would spend years in getting surgeries. As he approached adulthood, he finally told my parents that he didn't want any more. The scars had become a part of his persona. He was alive and well and didn't mind the scars. One of his legs was longer than the other and that caused him to walk with a little limp that was almost undetectable.

Everything in my life changed in those weeks after the accident. I learned a lot and I lost a lot. I, along with my family, survived.

THIS PAGE INTENTIONALLY LEFT BLANK.

Was there a traumatic event that you feel changed the course of your life?

MCGYVERISH

Carrot and I were at loose ends. I was recovering from surgery and was finally at a point where I was feeling pretty darn good. It had been more than a year since I had felt like doing anything other than sleeping and gluing my eyeballs to the television. She was there to be a caregiver to both me and her mother, who was also ill. I loved having my best and most trusted friend around.

Today was a good day, the sun was bright and my shiny white  convertible was calling to us. "Come to me," it was whispering lyrically; "Take me to the country"; it was teasing us, taunting us. The front grill seemed to have a warm welcoming smile. The red leather seats appeared as comfortable easy chairs. With the top down, that car was as sexy as Jessica Rabbit. Add some 1960's rock and roll and she was a complete package. There was no way we could resist.

We grabbed some sodas and CDs and we were soon settled into the bucket seats. We put the top down, slipped in some music, and off we went. We zipped out the driveway and onto the highway, passed through town and ended up on some back roads that would lead us towards Oroville. We had some deli sandwiches and fixings and planned to have a bit of a picnic near the reservoir. We found a spot and munched down our lunch.

As we left the reservoir, we decided to just take a road we had never been on before. We decided that at the first available road on the left we would start our adventure to wherever it would take us. The road was narrow and dusty without much pavement. It twisted and turned over dirt lined canals. We knew it would dead end at some point but decided to see how far it would take us. It seemed like miles. We saw no houses, no people, just trees, weeds and ditches with lots of trash. It seemed this whole area was being used as a trash dump for people who didn't want to pay for garbage pick-up.

I was getting tired. If you asked Carrot she would probably tell you I was also getting cranky. I needed to rest and wanted to get back to my bed. I stopped the car with the idea that Carrot would drive us home. But at just about the same time, the car heat indication went red and steam jetted out from under the hood. Uhh..Oh...

We were miles from anywhere. There was no way I could walk the distance to get back to the highway. I was getting panicky. Carrot was calm. She got out of the car and checked under the hood. A water hose had slit and we were losing coolant. She was so matter-of-fact that it irritated me. *How could she be so nonchalant about such a thing?* She told me we would have to wait for the engine to cool before she could fix it. *WHAT? Fix it? How in the world were we going to fix it? I don't take spare water hoses with me on random excursions to the country.* But, she simply said it would be OK – here, have the rest of your sandwich and – oh look – we still have some cream puffs. I sat in the passenger seat and obediently ate what she put in front of me.

After eating, I reclined my seat back and closed my eyes. Carrot went down the embankment to the trash lined ditch. She was so excited when she returned that I thought I could see her eyes twinkle. She had an old bicycle inner tube; pair of panty hose; some plastic grocery bags; a gallon milk jug; and a broken piece of glass. I thought to myself, *"She's lost it. I'm doomed out her in nowhere with a lunatic."* She started to explain to me how she was going to fix our problem but realized that I neither understood nor believed it was possible.

First, she used the broken glass to cut the legs from the panty hose, cut a piece off the already sliced rubber inner tube, and made strips from the bag. She wrapped the inner tube piece around the water hose and then wrapped one leg of the stocking around the patch. It was like a rubber patch held on with a panty hose bandage. She then took a piece of the grocery bag and wrapped that around the panty hose and covered it with a part of the other leg. She filled the gallon jug with water from the ditch and poured it into the radiator. After several trips for water, she told me to start 'er up!

The engine purred as Carrot inspected her handiwork. The temperature was staying at a safe degree and there were no visible signs of leakage. I looked at the hose in amazement. Carrot was a miracle worker! I would not die out on some dusty old road to nowhere!

We headed back toward home with the top down and singing hits from the 1960s at the top of our lungs. No heavy metal or rap for us, just tunes from our younger years.

Carrot was driving and I was enjoying the ride. As worried as I had been while parked alongside that ditch, I was just the opposite on the drive home. We pulled into our parking space, put the top up and popped the hood. There were no signs of leakage from the MacGyver type handiwork. The radiator had not lost any water.

As I settled down on my bed for a much needed nap, I wondered if Carrot had taken improv lessons from my mother.

THIS PAGE INTENTIONALLY LEFT BLANK.

To do with as you please.

WINDSHIELD WIPING

Morris Bartee knew how to fix almost anything. It was an inherited trait from his father and his father's father, and so on up the line. After all, he began life as a farmer's son on a working farm and shared chores with all of his brothers and sisters.

They didn't have a lot of money. In fact they were deeply in debt as was the case for most of the people during and after the depression. They made their own clothes, soap, furniture, pillows, etc. They grew vegetables and fruit and kept chickens for their eggs and meat. They bartered for beef and kept pigs for slaughter. They worked hard for what they had and appreciated everything they received for their hard work.

Part of appreciating what they had was not being too hasty to throw anything in the trash heap. If there was any way possible to repair any possession, that was what they did. Cars, truck, tractors to washing machines and stoves and anything else broken could be repaired. If they didn't have a needed part they made one up, they traded for it or they improvised by making something from something else. They were excellent improvisers.

Lois Reed, my mother was born with a silver spoon in her mouth. She had a maid who tidied her room and did her laundry. Doing dishes was not a concern for her. Instead she helped her mother tailor and repair women's clothing. She enjoyed doing the seamstress work especially for the high-society ladies whose pictures, adorned with her mother's handiwork, would show up in the newspaper. Sweeping and cleaning was not her thing.

Lois' father was a highway architectural engineer. During that time, only a few people in the Chicago area could put that title on their resume. He was paid a pretty penny and took all those pennies home to his family. He was not one to carouse. Instead he was a devout family man and his little girls were his pride and joy. Diamond ring gifts for graduation and mink coats for their 18th birthdays. Life was good at the Reed home in Harvey, ILL. If something was broken, it was simply replaced with something newer, bigger or/and better. Whatever it was, a new one would appear sometimes before Lois even realized it was broken.

When Lois Reed met and married Morris Bartee, everyone thought "Oh boy, don't see how this is gonna work!" But, to everyone's surprise, Lois quickly became used to using an outhouse, ringing the necks of chickens, baking bread, and sewing everyday clothing. Morris and the rest of the male Bartee's taught her how to check the water and oil in the car, change a flat tire, switch out the burned fuses, and replace the heating coil in the water heater. What they didn't teach her, she figured out on her own.

Lois learned the one most important thing about being a Bartee – how to improvise. She was a master at it. Within just a few years of marriage she became a down-to-earth, blue-jean wearing, tool wielding woman. And the Bartee's were also famous for their teasing so she made it a point that they would have nothing to tease her about. She became strong, formidable, and self-sufficient.

There was a special bond between Lois and her sisters-in-law. Since she had left her one and only sister back in Illinois and came to California to be with Morris, she latched onto the sisters who had taken her under their wing. She shared a special bond with Shirley, the wife of Morris' older brother. She had a similar background to Lois and they became a unit to reckon with.

One day, Lois and Shirley had to go somewhere. I don't remember where. It was important to get there even though I don't know why. They got into the only car available for them to drive and hoped they would be able to complete the errand before the heavy, dark clouds above opened up and released their loads of freezing rain upon them. There was no heat and the windshield wiper motor was not working. But, it was what they had at the time and if the rain started they would improvise.

Walnut Creek was about an hour away and the route was over Kirker Pass Road. In those days it was a long steep climb on what we would now consider to be narrow roads. The rain made the roads slick and cars never seemed to slow down to accommodate for the weather. The speed limit was 40 MPH and most people liked to take get their cars up to about 45 MPH before attempting the steep grade over the pass. The only other route option was Marsh Creek Road and that was long and tedious. The two women decided on Kirker Pass.

About the time they were leaving Pittsburg and headed up the Pass, the rain clouds started spewing heavy rain. The women pulled over and surveyed the situation. Shirley got out and checked to make sure the wipers still had usable rubber. She got back into the dry car and announced that the passenger side wiper was in good shape.

They sat and thought about the situation. Lois was looking through the miscellaneous things that had been haphazardly thrown on the floor of the back seat. But, found only a screw driver and pair of pliers.

After much discussion they came to a decision. Both women took the shoe laces out of their shoes. One started tying them together while the other went out and put the good wiper on the driver side. Then they tied the longest shoelace to the wiper with the shorter one just a bit further down the wiper. They pulled the long lace through the passenger side window and the shorter one through the driver side window.

When the windows become too wet for Lois, the driver, to see, Shirley would pull her shoelace which in turn pulled the wiper and scraped off the raindrops. Lois would then do her part by pulling the lace which would bring the wiper back and wiping the window in the other direction. And so they went... one pulling and then the next. They went all the way into Walnut Creek, took care of their business and returned home.

Morris and his brother were quite surprised when they returned home and found the women had accomplished their goal. There was some teasing mixed in with some irritation from Lois and Shirley that they had been left to drive an unsafe car. But in the end, it had all come out OK because the once, lily-white handed women had learned that everything can be fixed if you just used your imagination and improvised.

Morris never again scoffed when he returned home from work and found Lois tearing apart the washing machine or building bookshelves. Lois wasn't the only one who learned a lesson. Morris learned not to under-estimate the power of a woman.

DON'T ALL MEN?

When you grow up as the only female in a whole pack of males you tend to forget that not all men have the same talents as one another. I mistakenly assumed boys were born with the ability to change a tire, check the oil, refill the windshield wash and many other automotive related tasks.

When I started bugging my father about wanting my driver's license, he started setting up car maintenance training lessons for me. His theory was that I should not be on the road if I can't come to my own rescue if I was to have a flat tire or run out of gas. Actually, I think he just was putting off my going to DMV and getting my license.

Anyway, by the time I graduated from high school, I could change a tire, change the oil, use jumper cables, do the Coca Cola trick to clean the battery terminals, pop the clutch to start, check the spark plugs for loose connections, and other handy bits and pieces of information about cars. Still I did not get my license until I was in my early twenties!

Because I had to be "trained" in all this vital car repair stuff, it seemed to me that boys had it made because they just knew stuff. I had to learn it. I had to get it wrong a bunch of times before I could do all that same stuff that just came naturally to them.

When I left home I knew I would eventually find a man and "settle down." Besides the obvious emotional necessities (like love) I knew I was looking for a white collar guy with clean fingernails and a good vocabulary. It didn't occur to me (as it does not occur to many young ladies) that I should be looking for something "more" – even though I don't know what that "more" would be.

A very nice young man (an accountant) asked me out on a date to a fancy dancy restaurant for his company holiday party. I had the perfect cocktail dress -- red silk, strapless sheath, street length, trimmed with black velvet piping. I had designed and made the dress as part of a project in design school. I had received accolades as it came down the runway. It hugged my size 10 figure just the way it was supposed to do. I added some black suede heels. My roommates were impressed when I emerged from my room. I felt as beautiful as Jessica Rabbit.

My date picked me up promptly and we headed down to the visitors parking area where he had parked. The car seemed to be sitting a little lopsided, but I didn't say anything because I didn't want to embarrass him. He opened the door for me and we settled inside anxious to be on our way.

But, when he tried to back the car up, it wasn't going anywhere. The back driver side tire was flat. He got out and took a look. I got out and took a look. He ran his hands through his hair in exasperation and kept looking at the tire.

"Do you have a spare?" I asked. He said he didn't know if he did or not. A bit surprised at that, I said "Maybe you should check in the trunk and see if you have one." He opened the trunk and there was the spare, but he made no move to retrieve it. I waited. I didn't want to seem like a pushy know-it-all. After a while, I said "Are you going to change it?"

My date looked at me like I had just told him that roasted rats were on the company party menu. He looked physically ill. Sheepishly I asked, "Do you know how to change the tire?" I could tell from his face that he did not. "Do you want me to help you?" I asked quietly. He nodded his head.

Now. I want to be very clear. The LAST thing I wanted to do on that night was to risk ruining my delicately balanced ensemble by getting on my hands and knees and changing a dirty old tire. What man, in that generation would not know how to change a tire? And furthermore, where were his car repair DNA strands? He is a male, for goodness sakes, he should have been born knowing how to change a tire!

I kicked off my shoes and instructed him on how to get the tire out of the trunk. I proceeded to loosen the lug bolts and when they were on too tight I told him how to get them loose. The tire changing proceeded in that manner with me starting something and instructing him on how to finish it. When the chore was complete, I stood back and admired what we had accomplished.

My outfit was still good although it had a few extra wrinkles. My stockings had no runs. I put my shoes back on and got back in the car.

We missed the cocktail hour but arrived in time for dinner service. We never mentioned the flat tire to anyone – not even to each other. When we arrived back at my place; he walked me to the door; thanked me for helping him; told me he would give me a call; and left. I never heard from him again.

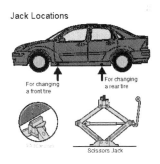

Jack Locations

For changing
a front tire

For changing
a rear tire

Scissors Jack

THIS PAGE INTENTIONALLY LEFT BLANK.

You can do nothing or anything with this space..

DON'T TOUCH THAT

It was 1979 and I had sent my kids to be with Mom and Daddy while I got ready for a move back to California from Connecticut. After the kids had gone, we moved from the house we were living in to a small apartment close to the base. We thought it would make it easier for Mike to help me with preparing for my trip.

I would drive across country with my two cats and camp as I went. I wanted to take my time because I was using a route I had never traveled before. Making the trip alone was not of much concern for me. I looked forward to the adventure.

Driving across country was nothing new to me. This would be the fourth time I had driven the 3,000 miles from the west coast to the east coast. The one thing I knew for certain was that my car must leave Connecticut in the best positive mechanical condition. I had a fairly new Chevy Vega which had never given me any problems in the year I had owned it. But, I wanted to have the oil changed, a tune-up, and the brakes and transmission checked.

My this time I knew that my husband was car mechanics illiterate and that his attempts to help me would only turn into complications. I knew a guy who was great at fixing cars and I asked him if he could do the tune-up. He agreed but he would not be able to do the oil change due to time restrictions. I told him that was OK because I could handle that task.

I drove the car up onto the ramps and laid out an old rug under the car. Then I got my oil change kit and placed it where I could easily reach it while under the car. Everything was going along smoothly when I heard a voice, "I was just wondering if you think it might be better if you waited for your husband to come home before trying to work on the car."

"I don't think so." I replied.

"What are you trying to do?" the gentlemanly voice asked.

"I'm changing the oil." I told him.

"Honey, I'm just trying to tell you that there is a lot of delicate parts under that car and it would be better if you let your husband handle it." He insisted.

Surely, this man did not know who he was talking to and anything about my husband's talents. I pulled the old oil filter canister off the car and the oil started streaming into the catch pan. I know had oil on my hands and forgot about that when I ran my fingers through my hair and then back across my forehead. It's a gesture I often use in frustration.

Still I did not emerge from under the car when I told him that I was well aware of the delicate parts under my car. I was getting ticked off at this man who seemed to have my car's best interest at heart.

"My husband knows submarines. He does not know a blooming thing about cars and if I let him under the car to make a repair, it would be a cold day in hell... honey."

"I don't mean to be disrespectful, but you're a young woman and you should not be under that car." He was getting ticked right back at me. I thought that this man has no right to tell me what to do with my car and I was becoming more irritated as the conversation continued. I needed to just let the oil drip out before replacing the filter and refilling the oil. So I pulled out from under the car to face the noisy old man.

"Oh dear," he said. "You're a bit of a mess." What I saw was an elderly gentleman dressed very neatly in khaki pants and a light blue polo shirt. He wore docker-type shoes and his blue socks matched his shirt.

"Sir, I do appreciate your concern however, I've been working on my own cars since I was in high school and I really know I can handle this. My husband knows nothing about cars. So if you would like to help by handing me tools, I will be most grateful. But, please do not under-estimate me because I don't have a penis." He was a bit shocked by the penis statement, but I didn't let that on that I noticed.

"I do think it would be best if I stayed just to make sure that you don't have an accident or anything." He had brought out a beach chair and set it up very close to where I had positioned the carpet.

There wasn't that much left to do, but I took my time. I wanted to let the man feel that he had, in fact, helped me. I asked for this and that tool and he handed each one to me.

As I was working he was explaining that back in his day, women didn't work on mechanical contraptions. That was considered to be men's work. Women were supposed to keep things running smoothing in the home.

I told, no I reminded him, that during the war years, women often took over the task of "men's work" because men were not around. Women worked in factories and became welders and construction workers. My own aunt was a big rig driver and mechanic. After doing all that they still went home to manage the house and take care of the kids. Women can and did do most things that men had traditionally done. When the wars were over, things went back to the way they were. But with each war, women were more reluctant to go back to being the silent party who was subservient to their male counterparts.

By this time I was refilling the oil and had my head under the hood. The nice gentleman was quiet for a long time and then said, "I think you're right. I forget that women have learned to take care of things themselves. But, for me, I'm happy my wife wouldn't dream of getting her hands dirty with the kind of thing you're doing today. She bakes and sews and takes care of me. I like that."

With my oil changing task complete, the oil properly disposed of; tools returned to the tool box, and the car purring smoothly when started, I thanks the gentleman for his assistance.

"I've gotta get back to my apartment. I have some bread dough rising and it's time to check on the rib roast. I still have to frost the cake I made earlier after I had done the laundry."

I left him standing in the parking lot as I closed my apartment door behind me. I wondered what he would tell his wife about me. I wondered what she would think about me changing my own oil. I also wondered why, when I saw how old he was, that I softened. I hoped that I had opened his eyes that women can, and in fact do, whatever they set their minds to and that it really isn't a new-age concept.

DISCRIMINATION

I always wanted to be where my Daddy was. It didn't matter where he was going or how long I would have to sit in the car while he was doing his business – I just wanted to be in his presence.

One day we went to look for a part for some piece of work equipment. We were in the car for hours, going from place to place. But we finally found it and Daddy said it was time to go put it into its place at work. But, he would drop me off at home before going to the work yard.

"Why can't I go to the yard with you? The boys get to go to work with you all the time. I want to go."

My father replied, "The yard is no place for a girl. It's dirty and there's no bathroom. I'll just take you home."

My father told my mother that he and the boys were going on an overnight tug boat tow trip. I begged my father to take me with them. I said I would cook and keep the galley clean. I promised not to be a bother and would stay inside the cabin the whole time. He didn't answer me. That was unusual because my similar requests had always been met with a negative response.

After a while my father told me I could go. But, I had to pay attention to what was being told and not to complain or say I wanted to come home. Once I was on the boat – that was it.

I did as I was told and cleaned the entire galley. I cooked a wonderful stew and corn bread. After dinner I laid on the galley "sofa" and feel sound asleep.

My mother asked how things went and my father said it was fine, but he didn't want to take me again. He said the galley was so clean that they couldn't find anything after I was gone. Also that everyone kept checking on me to make sure I was OK.

"Girls don't belong where men are trying to concentrate on work. It's too distracting. Girls belong at home."

When I was 16 I was excited about getting my driver's license (In CA you could drive at 16 back then). But, my father said NO. He said my grades would go down if I got my license. This didn't make sense to me because my brothers grades were beyond bad and he got his license. I didn't argue.

Two years before Daddy died, we had a long conversation about how I was treated differently from the many boys in our family. I was the only girl. I asked him why the rules were different for me. His answer was extremely honest -- *"Because you ARE different -- you're a GIRL! And because I treated you differently then, you are even more different NOW."*

How could I argue with logic like that?!

Mr. Frog walked into a bank carrying a ceramic sculpture. He sat down at Ms Patty Wack's desk and asked for a loan.

"We don't just give out loans to frogs," says Ms Wack. "Frogs don't have anything for collateral. Do you have collateral?"

Mr. Frog responded with "Why, yes. Yes I do. I have this lovely ceramic sculpture. It's an antique handed down to me from my grandmother."

Picking up the sculpture, Ms. Wack examined it up and down. She peaked inside through a little hole in the back. "Well, I don't think this would be sufficient collateral for a loan to a frog." Patty Wack said condescendingly.

"This is an outrage!" replies Mr. Frog. "It's clearly discrimination and I want to talk to the bank manager immediately!"

Ms Bank Manager appeared at the loan officer's desk in an instant. "What seems to be the problem?"

Ms Wack then explained that the frog wanted a loan and didn't have sufficient collateral. "We can't give loans to frogs. He just has the silly looking ceramic sculpture, if you want to call it that. I don't even know what this thing really is that he claims is so valuable."

Ms Bank Manager looked over the ceramic and thought a bit on the subject, she then stated:

"It's a nick-nack, PattyWack. Give the frog a loan."

THIS PAGE INTENTIONALLY LEFT BLANK.

Have you ever felt the sting of discrimination? Write about it here or just make some notes and write the story later.

COFFEE, BISCUITS AND STINKY CHEESE

It was 1990 and I was spending the holidays with my parents at home in Brentwood. A house that had once been filled with overflowing with sleeping children and extended family members, was eerily empty of youngsters. There was only my grandson peacefully sleeping in a real bed. In the past mattresses were thrown on the floor in an effort to accommodate the many little ones who were too excited to sleep for fear of missing Santa Claus.

Someone always gave my parents one of those boxes of sausages and cheeses over the holidays. My father saved them for Christmas day and set one aside for the two of us to share on Christmas morning. Our routine was to get up around 5 a.m., have coffee, and eat stinky cheese and crackers while fixing breakfast. It was OUR time. We talked about everything and anything. We gossiped and shared little stories. We laughed and reminisced. I had my father's complete attention and that didn't happen as often as I would have liked.

Christmas morning was when I could get Daddy's opinion about what I should do or what I should avoid doing. On this particular morning he was encouraging me to do everything I could to make my marriage work. He told me to have an oil change in my car and get a tune-up rather than put money into a new car. We talked about my job at Amtrak and how proud he was to have a "railroad" person in the family.

We ate the Limburger cheese and he mixed the biscuit batter for me. It was a happy morning. I was looking forward to more happy Christmas mornings. I reminded him of the times the kitchen was too full for us to have these conversations. It was when all my brothers and cousins brought their families to spend Christmas in this house. We are a family of early-risers and the kitchen would be filled with grown-ups laughing, joking and carrying on. It wasn't as personal for me and Daddy, but it was warm and packed with love.

I wanted the memories of previous holidays to be a reality in present time. I wanted Daddy's eyes to twinkle and Mom's big smile as they interacted with people they raised to adulthood. "Next Christmas let's invite EVERYONE here for Christmas like we did before. Let's have a big Christmas breakfast and lots of kids to get the presents." It was an innocent enough request – a longing for a repeat performance. I had spent so many holidays away from all my family. I wanted it, longed for it, and yearned for it. The entire demeanor of our morning shifted when my father replied:

"Well, I think you should do that if you want. It won't matter to me one way or the other." His tone was flat, kinda quiet. I asked if it was not what he wanted. "I won't be here." He said.

Astonished I asked "Why? Where on earth would you be if not at home?" He shrugged his shoulders and I saw a tear in his eye. He got up to pour me another cup of coffee and check on the doneness of the baking biscuits. He had health problems over the past year and I knew what he meant. I went to the bathroom and stayed there until I finished crying. By that time little Michael was awake and other family members had arrived. I was grateful for the distraction from our conversation.

The house was filling with the sounds of children. Presents were being handed out and Daddy and my brother, Richard, alternated at playing Santa. Mom and I finished preparing breakfast and we all sat down to finish up our Christmas morning.

That was the Christmas that my husband, Mike, entertained us with his attempt to help my Mom clean-up the kitchen. We laughed at him putting the garbage in the refrigerator and throwing out the bag of salad makings. In the afternoon, we drove to Mike's brother's house for Christmas dinner with Mike's family. Their dinners were far more formal than my families and the change was very pleasant.

As we made the hour long drive from one family to the other, I thought about the day. I thought about the cherished one-on-one Daddy time; my grandson opening his presents; my daughter hugging me; and the teasing from my brothers. It had been a good day, one that I would remember. But still… there was this little nagging thought that just wouldn't go away.

Christmas of 1991 played out far differently. My father died in September of 1991 which meant that his prediction had become reality. There was sadness over our home. My mother announced that she would be going to Indiana to spend the holidays with her side of the family. We encouraged her and knew our family had reached a major milestone in our lives.

It would take a lot more than a couple of Christmas holidays for our family to heal from the passing of our patriarch. And it would take a lot more than his loss to break us from being the family he groomed us to be and loose our sense of togetherness. Family. We were family. We would always be family and would always put family first. Yes. Christmas 1991 was a difficult one for us to manage. But, we talked to each other, cried with each other and reminded ourselves that at least we still had our family. That's what my father would have wanted. He would have expected us to lean on each other and make every Christmas forward be one centering on keeping the family whole and happy. He would expect the family to continue to grow and stay strong no matter how much we might miss him.

The legacy left was that the family wasn't just people related to you biologically, but rather we were related by those in our heart. Once a part of the family, we were always family. We may go our separate ways. We may get angry and disown each other. We may not see each other for years. But, here we are… still connected.

Even though our physical presence may not be in the same house, in the same kitchen, sharing coffee and jokes and anxiously waiting for the children to express delight at the gifts left from Santa. In our hearts, we are really all in the same place sharing the same thoughts.

Christmas has a different face for me now. Sometimes I'm alone at Christmas and sometimes I have a house of complete strangers combined with relatives. But I have the best Christmas ever when I allow myself to relive memories from so many delightful Christmas' from childhood and beyond. I am a very lucky and blessed girl.

Daddy and Bruce after opening gifts on Christmas morning.

A SANTA STORY

No one gets through childhood without the harsh glare of reality that the real Santa does not sit on a big red chair in the middle of a large department store. How absurd! Everyone knows he is really in his workshop at the North Pole working with the Elf's creating all those wonderful toys that are loaded into his big black bag. Just the idea that there may not even be a workshop is so disheartening that the child cringes at the mere thought.

During my days as a reporter for the local newspaper, I was assigned the task of writing an obit for a gentleman who died just a few days before Christmas. Harry Barker was the owner of a small auto garage in an eclectic area of town known as the "Village." He settled there as a young man, got married and raised four daughters, one of which, Susan, was a mechanic who worked with him in the garage.

I attended Mr. Barker's Christmas Eve memorial service. He was highly regarded in the community. He often extended credit on just a handshake. If a customer was in hard financial times, the bill simply got "lost" in the shuffle of paperwork on his desk.

I offered my condolences to Mrs. Barker. I told her I would pray that she would get through the holidays with wonderfully sweet memories. To my surprise, she looked up at me and said "Oh dear, I don't know what to do about Santa. What am I supposed to do?" I took her hand and tried to reassure her that everything would be OK. But she insisted, "Harry is gone and I'm the only one who knows! You have to help me." I tried to stay calm while trying to calm Mrs. Barker, but calming people down just wasn't my forte. I truly did not understand.

I asked her, "What can I do to help?" To my surprise she said, "There's a list. We have to find it." She grabbed my coat and tossed it to me as she hurried for the door. She stopped asked Susan for the shop keys as she tried to slip by her.

"Mom, let's wait and go to the shop in the morning. We have guests. Whatever is it, it can wait." Susan gently tried to redirect her Mother back toward the guests. But, Mrs. Barker was insistent. "No. There isn't much time. Susan." And with that we proceeded to walk the three blocks to the shop in confused silence.

Mrs. Barker searched through her husband's desk, opened all the cabinets, and then... in the back of the shelves, among countless Haynes auto repair books, she found what she was looking for -- an old-fashioned frayed green cloth account book. She opened the book and we saw 1956 written in large block numbers across the top of the page. Below the year there was a list of names and addresses in one column and a description of something in the second column. The book contained year after year of the same sort of list. The last entry was the current year, 1998, and, just like the other years, there was a list of names.

Mrs. Barker sat behind the desk with me and Susan waiting for an explanation. "Harry loved this community. He had such a big heart and felt so blessed to have so much in our lives. We really didn't want for much of anything. We had financial independence, beautiful girls, our life was full. Harry saw so much trouble in the lives of others and he was driven to give people help and hope."

"Mom, everyone knows how generous Dad was. It was no secret." Susan quietly reminded her mother.

Mrs. Barker continued, "You really didn't know. He wouldn't tell any of you girls that he wanted to be Santa Claus."

I sat in the old wooden chair listening and shades of clarity were beginning to form. "Mrs. Barker, are you saying that Harry acted as Santa to people outside his family?"

"Yes! Yes! He wrote down names all year long. These people were ones who had done some unnoticed good deed for someone else. Some of the people would have had difficulty providing Christmas dinner or gifts for their own children. He wrote them all down. Here. Right here." Like a fog that lifts in the afternoon sun, Susan and I could clearly see what Mrs. Barker was trying to tell us.

"Remember? After Christmas Eve dinner your father always had to go back to work for some reason or another? Yes, he went to the shop, but not to work. He put together baskets of things, food, toys, clothing, gift certificates, and maybe even a small tree. Then he took them around to the different houses on his list and dropped them at the front door. Sometimes he'd do a 'ring and run' thing. Sometimes, he'd call them anonymously from the shop and tell them to go to their front door. If was so much fun for him and he was always exhilarated when he returned home."

Mrs. Barker and Susan decided not to let Harry's tradition die. They took over his identity of Santa Claus and although Harry was gone – Santa was not. I helped them load the baskets and deliver them to the names on the list.

It was revealed to me at a very young age by my older brother and cousins, that Santa was really my parents. I was devastated. If there was no Santa, there was no hope of me ever getting anything I really wanted at Christmas. But, on the Christmas Eve of 1998 at the age of 34, I learned that there really was a Santa Claus named Harry.

The reality is that there are probably a lot of real-life Santa's out there, but mostly Santa is in the heart of everyone who believes in the good of other people.

THIS PAGE INTENTIONALLY LEFT BLANK.

HOME FOR THE HOLIDAYS

Lucille sat at her computer terminal desperately trying to keep her imagination in check. She looked over her right shoulder and grimaced at her overflowing in-box. The work wasn't going to be done by the midnight fairy and unless she could regain her focus, it wouldn't be done by her either. She finished up the current document and reached over for the next item.

This was only the first of November and she had another whole month until her vacation over the Christmas holidays. Her body and brain were crying out for an extended break from computers, commuters, and complaints. She was anxious for a relaxing interlude on a Mexican beach far from the stressful city. But instead of her mind focusing on white sand and Margaritas, she kept drifting back to last year's vacation at her family home in Virginia.

Unable to concentrate on the flashing little line on the computer screen, Lucille thought back to her previous vacation and remembered the apprehension she experienced about visiting her family. Everyone was expressing concern for her mother, Maggie, living alone in the big country farmhouse where she and her siblings grew up. It was the first Christmas since her father's passing. As the memories came flooding back, Lucille could almost feel the crisp air bite at her nose and smell the oak burning in the fireplace. What should have been a peaceful rest in the country turned into a mad-house mouse race.

Her older sister, Janine, had picked her up at the airport. Lucille hadn't been home in many years and she felt a bit unsettled as the old run-down building that once housed local model airplane clubs and sky divers, had been replaced by a thriving international airport. The growth of the airport mirrored the growth of the community. The hometown atmosphere seemed lost in an avalanche of people, businesses and shopping malls.

Lucille spotted Janine and her two twin daughters almost immediately. After the hugs and greetings, they all piled into Janine's station wagon and head towards the James River Bridge. Traffic was slow but that gave the women time to chat and get caught up on family gossip. They decided to stop for something to eat along the way.

Just across the bridge there was an old country store with everything from gasoline to hunting supplies. At the back of the store was a restaurant serving country-style food such as collards and barbeque topped with cole slaw. The restaurant was nearly empty so they had no problem finding a booth large enough to accommodate all four of them.

"It's comforting to know that some things never change," sighed Lucille as she remembered the building from her childhood days. She looked around at men in quilted wool plaid over shirts and ball caps. The men were standing in line with six-packs of beer and bags of chewing tobacco. "On the other hand, it would be nice if some things actually did change." Lucille turned back around to her sister.

"So tell me the family poop? Any good gossip?" Lucille and Janine had always been the closest of the kids. They were in-tune with each other's lives and even the long separations couldn't seem to drive a wedge between them. They often had long talks on the telephone between visits home.

After a brief run-down of who left who for whom and who is in trouble with the law, etc. etc., the talk turned more serious.

"It's Mom" Janine said. "Since Dad's death she has really gone downhill."

"Downhill? How steep of a grade is this hill?" Lucille asked.

"She's just not the same. The house is a mess, newspapers everywhere, dirty dishes, and I don't think she has changed the sheets in about three weeks when I came to do the laundry for her. She doesn't seem to care about anything anymore. Well... except Wheel of Fortune and American Idol." Janine's words left Lucille scowling.

"What should we do? Hire a housekeeper? What? You know she won't leave that house so living with any of us would be out of the question." Lucille asked.

Janine further explained that their mother wasn't keen on the idea of having a stranger clean the house. "That's not the worst of it. The house has become infested with mice." She continued to tell Lucille that they were not the kind of little mice that ran over their toes when they were on the potty as kids. These mice were big and practically set themselves a place at the dinner table.

Lucille flashed back to the days when her feet wouldn't touch the floor when sitting on the toilet. She would purposely stay in the bathroom, staring at the mouse hole next to the bathtub and hoping one of them would run out so she could get a glimpse of the furry little creature. One day she got her wish but the mouse startled her so much that she let out a shriek and scared it back into the hole.

The rest of the trip was short and quiet with Lucille gazing out the window at the familiar countryside. No matter how populated the north side of the James River became, there still was a country atmosphere to the south. She loved the relaxed attitude of the country especially after being surrounded by hectic activity in her city home in California.

After two days of visiting relatives and friends, Lucille was finally able to have a chance to brooch the subject of her mother's housekeeping. She chose her words carefully.

"Mom, I was wondering if you would mind if Jan, Katie and I did a little tidying up for you. I thought that since the whole family is going to be here on Christmas Day that we could do some decorating and fill the house with some holiday cheer. Would that be OK with you?"

Her mother's eyes lit up at the thought of having the entire family in the big old farmhouse again. "Of course it would be OK. That will give me time to do some cooking. We need to make out a menu."

As soon as Lucille got confirmation, we sent a message to both her sisters to get to their mother's house. The text read: *Hurry here. Must clean kitchen. Mom's cooking.* The idea of their mother preparing food in a kitchen containing mouse droppings was not acceptable. Since Lucille's arrival they had been eating out or people had been bringing food over, so there was no fear of eating contaminated food.

Less than an hour later, all the girls were on the front porch where they made a plan. Katie would take Mom Christmas and food shopping while the other two cleaned the kitchen from top to bottom. They decided to call on their Aunt Lee for reinforcement. Aunt Lee would be at the house when the shoppers returned and ask to help with wrapping the gifts. Between the shopping and wrapping, Mom would most likely be out of the kitchen for the entire day.

At the end of the day, the girls stood back and surveyed their success. Every dish had been washed and replaced in cabinets and drawers that were sanitized and lined with "pest repellent" type paper. Anything that was not in a sealed container was disposed of and replaced with freshly bought ingredients. The pantry was now lined with labeled plastic containers all lined up neatly in a row. The kitchen smelled like a mixture of bleach and a bright spring day. One room down and a whole house to go.

But, they were still concerned about the mouse issue. Just cleaning the kitchen would not stop them from returning to the scene of their crime. They did not want to use mouse traps that would have to be emptied and re-set. Nor did they want to use a poison that might leave a decaying rodent in the walls. They went looking for a better mousetrap and ended up with an exterminator who was willing to come out that same day.

"Sure I cun git rid a 'em. I know yer Mama fer long time and happy ta help. My wife passed last spring. Wuld be great if she would throw in a home cooked meal ever once a while. I'd really give deep discount for that." Roger Evans was a member of their family church and the girls knew and trusted him. He was a tall man who looked like he had spent his life as a cowboy rather than an exterminator. When he smiled his blue eyes twinkled. He was a happy man and the loss of his wife had not changed his positive attitude.

An agreement was made and their Mom seemed more than pleased to have Mr. Evans come to her home every other day to control the pest and rodent problem. She also was delighted to have someone to share her cooking and meals with. It looked as through the collaboration between Mr. Evans and Maggie would work out just fine.

The girls continued to clean the house managing to complete one or two rooms a day. After a week, they were done. The house had a renewed freshness and truly felt like home once again. Aunt Lee suggested a woman from church as a housekeeper. Since the woman was already someone that their mother knew, it might be easier to convince their Mom to have her help.

Church was something that it seemed had been pushed aside since their father's death. The girls and their children and husbands asked if they might accompany Maggie to church on the next Sunday.

It took some coaxing, but she finally agreed. The plan was that during the coffee hour after the services, they would invite Mrs. Smith to join them. They would manipulate the subject towards the housekeeping and Mrs. Smith would eventually ask if Maggie if she would consider letting her come over and do some dusting and sweeping. Mrs. Smith, a woman in her mid-30s, did housekeeping to supplement the family income. Mr. and Mrs. Smith had been saving up to buy a house, so every little bit of extra work helped. Maggie was happy to be of assistance to the young woman and agreed to let the woman come over twice a week to "tidy" up.

It was Christmas morning and Lucille awoke to the smell of fresh baked homemade cinnamon rolls and coffee. She stretched under the covers and smiled to herself as she realized that she was completely relaxed and comfortable. This was home. This was where she could rejuvenate her cells and gain prospective on her life. She was happy.

The family began arriving and the house quickly filled up with laughter and squeals of children. Everyone brought at least one dish to add to the bountiful feast that Maggie had prepared. Presents were opened followed by hugs and thank you all around. Maggie invited Roger Evans for dinner as well as the Smith family. They didn't stay long, but it was good to see them mix in with the family.

After the commotion had settled down, the children and husbands returned to their own homes, and a soft quiet returned to the farmhouse, the girls brought in their own special gift for their mother. Each girl had a pet carrier and each carrier contained a cat. Katie's cat was a long-haired calico with a collar identifying the cat as **Rainbow**. Janine presented a Maine coon male cat with a leather collar inscribed with the name **Brutus**. Katie's gift was a female orange tabby kitten of less than one year old named **Lucy**. All cats were purported to be excellent "mousers" and all had been spayed, neutered and vaccinated.

Maggie's husband did not like cats, but they had always had a dog. Spike was the current canine family member. He was old and mostly spent the day sleeping. But when Lucy jumped on him, he came to life and chased the cat around the house. Later on, they were sleeping side by side in Spike's bed.

"Lucille? Lucille... there's a rush file that needs to go out right away." The voice snapped her out of her warm memory place in Virginia and back to reality in San Francisco, California. The computer was still flashing that little line and the pile of files were mounting up in her box. She glanced over at her calendar. It still showed one whole month before vacation time. Ugghhh...

The days passed faster than she had thought they would. She had packed her bikini and flip flops and was ready for that Margarita on the beach. But something had changed. Lucille's supervisor informed her that she had gone over the five year time frame and was not eligible for an addition week of vacation. If she did not take it before January 1st, she would lose that year's week. It was a delightful surprise for Lucille because she could use an extra week in the sun.

As she lay in the beach, baking her skin to a nice brownish tan, sipping on her umbrella drink, and munching on nachos, her mind kept going back to the subject of mice, cats, her sisters and Maggie's cinnamon rolls. She picked up her laptop and checked on flights from Acapulco to Newport News, VA. Next she called the front desk of her resort to tell them she would only be staying ONE week instead of three.

"Jani? Hey there! I was wondering if you could do something for me. Can you pick me up at the airport on Monday?"

Lessons Learned

When a person says "I live on a compound" the image that instantly comes to mind is one of a devout religious cult that lived behind a locked fence where strangers were not welcome or allowed. That's not always the case.

From the ages of two to five years, I lived on a compound. Part of the property included access to the Dutch Slough, a river along with other rivers that surrounded Bethel Island. The back of the property was bordered with a farm and there were neighbor houses on the two other sides. It was a huge piece of land, probably about 10 acres. There was only one fence and it was there to keep the neighbors cows from visiting us. The land was not enclosed nor did it have an ominous feeling to visitors.

It was a beautiful place to live with Willow and Oak Trees dotted throughout the landscape. In the open areas there were man-made fishing ponds that were planned to be used for people who come to the river to fish, but are not lucky enough to get a catch. The ponds simplified the fishing experience and increased the odds of going home with a sizeable number of fish for the grill.

My father, his brothers and my grandfather were cleverly inventive individuals. Now-a-days you would call them DIY'ers with renewable or repurposed materials. They bought the land and the next issue was housing for each of the families. The end of World War II meant there was an abundance of military surplus items being sold on the cheap. They bought four Quonset Huts and refurbished them for use as three residences and a workshop. As you came down the driveway, my grandparents' house was on the right, my uncle's house was the first house on the left, next to that was the workshop and next to that was our house. The workshop still exists to this day but it is surrounded by campsites since the property has been converted to a resort.

I was so very young, it really didn't matter much to me about the house. It was where my mother, father and brother were, so that's all I needed. I didn't much care for sharing a room with my brother and having to use the outhouse was a bit uncomfortable. But, we made do and I was happy there.

Because we lived in a somewhat protected area, I was free to roam around the property at will. I'm sure that between all the family members, I was supervised more than most children my age but I just didn't notice it. I also didn't realize that I was enjoying a freedom that could only be found by virtue of living on a compound.

On warm days I would jump off the front porch and wander around looking at everything I could see. I went to the fish ponds and watched the frogs hop on the Lilly pads. The spiders spun intricate webs that looked like tiny diamonds had been woven into them from the morning dew. I made a stop at Grandma's for hot "coffee milk" which was simply hot milk with enough of a splash of coffee to give it some coffee flavor. Then it was off to my uncle's where Aunt Shirley always had wonderful cakes that were the perfect accompaniment for the coffee milk. With my tummy full, I ventured over to the shop where I would sometimes find my father, uncle or cousin working on a project. They would explain what they were doing, and sometimes I understood, but most times I just said "that's good" and continued on my adventure.

Between the workshop and our house were several large concrete conduit pipes stored and lined up neatly in a row. I could stand completely upright in them. I would pretend they were some sort of house and play in them for hours. One day I found a Mama cat with her kittens sleeping in one of the pipes. We had many feral cats who kept the mice at bay, so they were all treated with respect. I didn't touch the kittens because they were too little and I remember being told that if you touch them the mother will leave and never come back. I ran back to my house and brought back some milk and cat food. Mama seemed to appreciate the gesture and purred for me.

After that discovery, I came back every day with milk and food and when it seemed they were old enough I held each kitten and gave them all names. I was warned that they were not pets, but rather "working cats" who would not do their job if I continued to feed them. I worried about that, but still did not stop feeding them. We often left small amounts of food out for the feral cats. The idea was that they would not starve to death, but be hungry enough to hunt.

One day, I went to the pipe and there was a dead mouse among the kittens. Mama came to me and rubbed up against me asking for praise for the gift she had left for me. I was ecstatic! I now knew that even though I had feed them they would still hunt and kill mice.

As the days went on, I went to the pipe less and less and each time I did go a kitten would be absent. By that time they were full size and able to fend for themselves. Mama left and eventually all but one kitten was gone. I begged my mother for us to take the kitten in and after much pleading, my request was granted. I don't remember the name of the kitten and it was seldom really around. But it came when I called the name and loved my attention.

I learned a couple of valuable lessons during my time with the kittens. I learned that every living thing has a job, a purpose for being alive. I also learned that as time progresses I may gradually lose interest in whatever had my complete attention earlier. And, even though you may show a baby living thing love and attention, eventually it will grow up and leave to have a life on its own. Also, sometimes, if it loves you enough, it will stay with you.

Late in the summer of that year, I spent a couple of weeks with my aunt in her mountain home. When I returned there was a life-size doll lying on the sofa. I ran to pick it up and play with it. Everyone was yelling at me as I reached for the doll. Just then the doll flinched and opened its eyes and then a cry came from the mouth. It was a REAL baby!! Oh how exciting it was! Mom let me hold him and then later I gave him a bottle. I knew I loved this little creature. I loved him more than the frogs on the lily pads; more than coffee milk and cake; and, more than the kittens in the pipe.

As I sat in the big rocking chair, holding my brother in my arms and trying desperately to make the chair actually move in a rocking motion, I wondered – would this perfect little creature grow up and leave me? I was sure that his purpose was to give me something to love since the kittens were gone. I was also sure that I'd never lose interest in anything he did. But, will he love me enough to stay with me?

Over the years, two more brothers were added to our family and each was just as special as the one I found on the sofa when I was five years old. More lessons from having them in my life – even if you leave a brother or they leave you, they will always be with you. There is a bond that can never be broken. A love you can always count on. I've been blessed with four brothers and I know there will never be a time when I won't be loved.

GIFTS FROM FURRY FRIENDS

May 2012 was a pivotal point in my life. Mike had a heart attack and was a patient at the heart institute in Greenville, NC. I was living in the country house in Tyner. I loved the floor plan of that house and was quite comfortable there without any other human. I really wasn't ALONE. I had Jade, my dog, and Jax, my cat. They were better companions than any two-legged roommate could ever be.

Of course, the solitude was very welcome after three years of constantly cleaning up household messes created by an end-stage alcoholic. I had a giant size housekeeping chore ahead of me, but it was less of a problem since I could tackle the situation without the possibility of my efforts only lasting a few hours. I could clean at my own pace and be as thorough as I deemed necessary.

There were other things I could do on my own terms. I could cook when I wanted and what I wanted. I took long walks around the pastures and sat under the apple tree throwing tennis balls for Jade to chase. I would take as many baths in a day that I wanted. Sometimes I even sipped on a glass of wine while covered in bubbles. I watched television in the living room rather than my bedroom. Things were different and I embraced that difference.

Jax the Max Cat

I'm not a fearful person. The fact that I had no real neighbors didn't bother me. I didn't wake up in the middle of the night and cower under the covers because I heard a bump outside my bedroom window. Maybe I should have been afraid, but I just wasn't.

Jade and Jax were acutely aware of the changes in the house.

Sweet Girl Jade

Jade never left my side. Jax, being a bit lazier, slept in whatever room I was in. They were attentive and showed affection in many ways. Sometimes, I could have done with a little less affection.

They were free to come and go as they passed through the doggie door and they took advantage of that freedom every day. One day I returned from visiting Mike in the hospital and found some things tipped over on the kitchen counter. I thought Jax must have gotten up there and done some mischief. Just as I was about to give him that mean look, some quick movement caught my eye. It was a bird trying desperately to find a way out of the house. Oh… I see… you've brought me a bird, I thought. I reached down

and praised them both for being such good providers. I then managed to encourage the bird out the door and be on its way. Jax and Jade starred at me in horror as I set their prize free to the outside world after they worked so hard to get it for me.

The next morning started the same as my newly created routine: get up; take shower; brush teeth; etc., etc. after which I found my way to the coffee pot. I just happened to look down to see a dead mouse on the kitchen floor. Jax took ownership of that gift and purred as he wound himself in and out of my ankles. OH! Thank you, I told him… you're such a good hunter.

That night, I was awakened by some commotion on my bed. There was rustling and jumping and racing. I opened my eyes to find Jax and Jade both attempting to corral a  frog that one of them had brought in from the outside. This was just beyond any acceptable gifting routine. I got the frog and put it outside. Once again I got the "Awwww…. Mom…." Kind of reaction. But, they both settled down and we all finished up with a good night sleep.

The next morning, I was going to visit Mike. As I was driving out of the driveway, I wondered what new and exciting treat I would find waiting for me. I don't know why Jade and Jax were so intent on providing for me during that time. Maybe they sensed that Mike was gone and that they had to make up for his absence. Maybe they thought I had gotten rid of Mike and in order to avoid the same plight, they must show their worth. For me their worth was far beyond anything they could have brought to me.

When I returned home, I was pleased that there was nothing waiting for me in the kitchen. But after hearing strange sounds coming from the den, I discovered a live baby rabbit hiding under the easy chair. Oh boy… how long could this go on? Well… over the next few weeks there were lizards, mice, birds, rabbits, bones dug from some forgotten cache in the yard, and many other treasures. It seemed never-ending and I was a bit afraid they might try for a snake.

A couple of months and after lots of presents from my furry four-legged children, I packed up the country house and moved back to the Outer Banks to live with the grandkids. We would be in a temporary house for a month, so Jade went to stay with some friends in the country and Jax took up residence with my daughter.

Jade came home to us after we moved to what we thought would be our "permanent" home. Mike was back at home and Jade did not bring me any gifts on a regular basis. Jax decided to stay with Lisa and continued to bring her little surprises which she didn't hold as fond of an appreciation for as I did.

I missed waking up to surprises and seeing them delight in watching my reaction. I don't know why they thought it necessary to supply me with those treats – but it felt special to me that they went to all that trouble. I don't know if they thought – Mike is away and it's time to play or if it was their form of providing. Whatever. As much as it was a pain in my pa-tutti, I still miss it.

FROM THE MOUTHS OF…

Baby Brain: *Watch me flip.*

Me: *No, baby, the floor is too hard.*

Baby Brian: *I'll break my head open?*

Me: *If you fall you might hurt your head because the tile is very hard.*

Baby Brian: *My head break and my batteries fall out?*

Me: *Yes. Your batteries will fall out.*

ა ა ა

Me (age 7):   *Mama, please have another baby.*

My mother: *Babies are a lot of work.*

Me: *I'll help you if you have a baby.*

My mother: *How will you help me?*

Me: *I'll tell you when it cries.*

ა ა ა

Seven youngsters were all piling into the back seat and back-back area of a 1973 Ford Pinto station wagon. They ranged from 2 to 8 years of age. Carrot and I were taking them to the park. This was back in the day of no seat belt requirements and you could hold a baby on your lap in the front seat.

As we were accustomed to doing, before the key went in the ignition, we did a head count. Everyone knew to be quiet during this process. (1.. 2.. 3.. oh, I missed Jen.. 4.. 5.. 6.. and the baby makes 7 – ok we're good to go.).

Just as the count was getting to seven, a tiny voice from somewhere in the back issued a frim warning:.

"Hold on, Aunt Linda is driving."

ややや

After connecting with some "long ago" (didn't want to say OLD) friends, many memories -- some good -- some not so much have also been re-connecting in my brain. I've been pretty successful at finding some people I haven't heard from in decades. Because of that, Mike believes I can find ANYBODY so he's given me a list of old shipmates he wants me to find.

Me: *Mike, Master Chief Whoever is dead.*

Mike: *That can't be right, check again.*

I do love a challenge, but I still can't undo dead.

ややや

Gary stood at his brother's side and said "Oootic" and his brother, Bruce, handed him a Q-tip.

"No! Oootic!" the 3-year-old said again. His older brother replied with "OK. This is a Q-tip, see?"

Starting to get frustrated, Gary, yelled, "NO! NO! Dis fuzzy!" He promptly started pulling the entire cotton tip off the stick. "NO FUZZY!"

The older brother was baffled and couldn't believe Gary was so adamant about the Q-tip. He went to get his oldest brother, Richard, and the two of them calmed Gary down and then asked him to show them what he wanted. They were in the bathroom looking into the bathroom closet. Richard picked Gary up in his arms and said, "Show me."

Now Gary was furious, tears streaming down his cheeks, he wrestled out of Richard's arms and ran to the kitchen. Once there he pointed to a cabinet. "OOOTIC, OOOTIC!"

Once in the kitchen, Richard and Bruce looked at each other and knew in an instant what the baby wanted. They opened the cabinet and reached inside. Richard, always a teaser, slowly pulled out a toothpick from its little box. "Is this what you want?" Richard knew it was, but held the precious toothpick just out of Gary's reach.

"Yes! Yes!" Gary cried. Richard handed him the toothpick, After Gary gave his big brother a hug, it dawned on Richard... why does a three-year-old want or need a toothpick?

Me: *Do you want to go to Happy Steak?*
Carrot: *Yes*
Me: *Did you take a diet pill?*
Carrot: *Yes*
Me: Well, we better hurry before it kicks in

Upon being introduced to a six-year old little girl...
Lisa: *What do you want to be when you grow up?*
Girl: *A mermaid*

Lisa: *Is there something else you'd like to be if that doesn't work out?*

Girl: *Yes, a princess or a fairy.*

Lisa: Well, it's always good to have a backup plan.

♂♂♂♂

Pearls of Wisdom:

Hannah: *If things don't change they're gonna stay the same.*

Bruce: *A fish wouldn't get caught if it didn't open its mouth.*

Linda: *Knowledge is the key to survival.*

Mom: *Old age ain't for sissies and golden years ain't so golden.*

♂♂♂♂

Four kids under the age of six sat in a group admiring Brian's new puppy. It was a white puppy of undetermined parentage that had been rescued from a trip to the pound.

Kid 1:   *Look, it has a lot of fleas crawling around.*

Kid 2:   *Let's pick them off and put them in a jar.*

Brian: Oh yeah… we can take them to the flea market!

♂♂♂♂

How Carolyn became Carrot:

Adult   *Why are you crying?*:

Baby: *Wan a carrot*

Adult hands the baby a carrot.

Baby: *No.* (cries harder) *Carrot!*

114

Carolyn enters the room.

Baby holds out arms to her: *A Carrot!*

Adult: *OH! You want Aunt Carrot!*

Baby is now happy in Carrot's arms.

જ⊱⊱⊱

Lois loved having a big garden, she used a quarter of an acre every spring so that she could have lots of fresh vegetables. She was meticulous about preparing the ground before planting. After Morris tilled the area, Lois followed by raking through the clumps..

The summer after Richard and Carolyn married, Lois invited her new daughter-in-law to join her in the annual garden. They would work the garden together and then Lois would teach Carolyn the fine art of canning and preserving.

Carolyn showed up at Lois' house and the two began working fertilizer into the soil. They were on their hands and knees and had their bare hands kneading the smelly stuff into the soil.

They hadn't said to much in the past hour. It was obvious that Carolyn was having some misgivings about their task. She was working very slow and was wiping her hands on a rag almost after every handful. She kept looking over at Lois and wanting to ask a question.

A realization finally came to her. "WAIT!!! This stuff is SHIT!" she screamed out. She stood up in disgust and glared at Lois. Lois was laughing so hard she could barely respond. She handed an empty fertilizer bag to Carolyn and pointed out the words "equine manure".

Now they were both laughing. Carolyn washed her hands and grabbed a pair of work gloves. They enjoyed a wonderful harvest that year.

❧❧❧

Linda went to visit her 90 year old uncle in the hospital. He had emphysema and was oxygen.

Uncle Al: *Poodlepop, could you light me up a cigarette?*

Linda: *Uncle Al, you know I can't do that. You can't smoke in here.*

Uncle Al: *I know but if you just wheel this thing out into the back stairs, no one would know.*

Linda: *You want me to push your bed out to the landing?*

Uncle Al: *You're strong. You can do it.*

Linda: *I'm not going to help you smoke while you are on oxygen and in the hospital.*

Uncle Al: *OK. Then help me break out of this joint.*

Uncle Al

LET ME EXPLAIN

I love the **SWAPORTUNITY** commercials on TV. It reminds me of Bruce, when his kids were very young, he would go into long-winded, complicated and absurd explanations of something that was really very simple.

They kids listened intently trying to understand the elaborate explanation. The oldest daughter would look up at him after hanging onto his every word while her brain was trying to take it all in. Then it would hit her that he was pulling her leg! She'd lift her head at an angle and look right into his blue eyes, wrinkle up her forehead and say "Nuhht naw -- that's not real!!"

Bruce would smile that crooked smile and his blue eyes would twinkle. He'd raise his eyebrow and kinda give a wink. But, he never acknowledged that he was being absurd. He just let the kids wonder... and wonder... until they figured it out for themselves.

Bruce – Be careful of what lurks behind that smile!

EASTER QUERY

I've always had a problem with completely understanding the non-religious aspects of the Easter holiday. Here are some things I just don't get:

1 -- I'm not sure what the rising of Christ has to do with eggs, candy or baskets.

2 -- Why does a rabbit bring eggs? Why doesn't a chicken bring them?

3 -- Why do women and girls wear Easter bonnets? Why not just wear a hat or nothing on their head at all?

4 -- What is the reason for coloring the eggs?

5 -- What about the lamb? How does a baby lamb relate to rabbits, chickens, eggs, candy, baskets?

6 -- Why do we send our little children to go gather eggs in a field where they could get stung by bees or bit by a snake?

7 -- Why does my husband wear bunny ears all day on Easter Sunday when he doesn't wear a tail?

8 -- Do the Playboy Bunnies get the day off or are they all out hiding eggs?

9 -- Is it OK to wear white shoes on Easter Sunday since the holiday is before Memorial Day?

10 -- Why do we dress our kids in fancy outfits when they are just stain the new clothes with chocolate and candy slobber?

11 -- Why doesn't the Easter bunny come down the chimney like Santa Claus? There's less of a chance for a fire to be in there on Easter than on Christmas?

12 -- If we are trying to teach our children to live healthier lives, why not use carrots instead of candy?

These are just a few of the questions for which I have never been given satisfactory answers. Can anyone help me with this?

WILLIAM'S LIFE STATION

She was the most beautiful woman he had ever seen. Her shiny coppery red hair and bright blue eyes reminded him of a story book character. William knew he loved her from the first moment he saw her. When she talked to him she was cool, aloof, and he wondered if he could ever be worthy of her.

One day William took a chance and stopped by Roseanna's house. He didn't really want to see her so much as wanting to have a conversation with her father. His intent was to ask permission to court Rosanna. Dressed in his best shirt, slacks and a straw hat in his hand, he shifted from foot to foot when he saw her father reaching for the front door knob.

Mr. Miller was a tall stately man and William felt dwarfed standing next to him. William was not tall, but stood a healthy 5'11". William extended his hand to Mr. Miller who returned with a firm handshake. William explained that he had come to ask permission to court Roseanna.

After an exchange of questions and answers, Mr. Miller set some goals for William to achieve before he could officially start courting his daughter. Mr. Miller believed, as a good father would, that Rosanna deserved only the best suitor who had the means to provide the best possible life for her. Mr. Miller required William to show his ability to improve his station in life. Once that was accomplished, he told William that they would talk again about the possible courtship of Rosanna.

Lumberton Company had never had a purchasing manager — only a clerk. Mr. Oakley had never seen a need for a manager when he had young William on the job. The youngster was eager, competent, honest and reliable. No need for a manager. But, William didn't want to stay a clerk because he was focused on improving his life station and that meant he needed to make more money which, in turn, would raise his status. William set an appointment with Mr. Oakley's secretary. She insisted that William didn't need an appointment to talk to his boss, but William explained that he needed to present himself with as much professional prowess as possible. He explained his plight with wanting to court Roseanna Miller and the secretary, who was in a romantic state of mind, scheduled William for the next morning. Before he left the office, the secretary advised him to bring bear claws – Mr. Oakley loved bear claws.

William arrived 10 minutes early. He sat on the edge of the upholstered straight back chair with his box of bear claws on his lap. He wore his finest dress pants, a white and blue pin-striped shirt and a blue bow tie. His shoes had been buffed to a mirror shine. In his mind, he looked the part of a manager.

Mr. Oakley entered the vestibule and went straight through to his office shutting the door behind him. In less than a minute, he re-opened the door and said "What's in the box?" William responded with just two words "Bear Claws". Mr. Oakley pulled the door wide open and invited William in followed by a request from the secretary for two cups of black coffee. He hesitated for just a second turn to William and said "You do drink it black, right son? Of course you do." Motioning to a chair at the little side table, William was invited to sit. "So what's this all about William?"

The secretary quietly entered the room and placed a cup of coffee in front of each of the men. She then took the box of bear claws and left the room but she almost instantly returned with the pastries neatly arranged on top of a paper doily which rested on a beautiful crystal plate. She put two linen napkins in front of each man. Then she disappeared so silently and quickly that it was almost as though she was never in the room.

"Well, sir, I've been working for you for five years now," William began his speech that he had practiced in front of the mirror. He went on to plead his case for advancement to Purchasing Manager from a mere clerk. He explained to his boss that he must improve his station in life in order to court, let alone marry, Miss Rosanna Oakley.

Mr. Oakley looked at him askance with his mouth full of bear claw. "Your 'station in life'? What exactly do you mean by that?"

William thought for a moment and realized that he didn't know the answer to Mr. Oakley's question. "I'm not exactly sure, sir. But, I'm thinking that it means that I must make more money, increase my responsibility here and become a more productive member of the community." He told him about his agreement with Mr. Miller and that if William met the terms of the agreement, he would be allowed to court his daughter, Roseanna.

"Hmmmm, I see," said Mr. Oakley. "Are you asking for a raise? Because you make very good money as a purchasing clerk and I'm hesitant to hand you a raise so that you can just use it to go on fancy dates with a woman who feels she is above you in class."

"OH, no! No! Mr. Oakley, you have the wrong idea about Roseanna. She's sweet and caring. She's not at all the kind of woman you describe. I believe if I can afford it, she will marry me once she really has a chance to get to know me. I'm sure that her father just wants to be sure she marries someone with ambition and aspirations of having a good life. Besides I'm not asking for just a raise for no reason." William spoke quickly but concisely. He wanted to be sure that Mr. Oakley understood his situation.

"Oh? How do you see this raise happening?"

William answered, "I would like a change in position, a promotion if you will. I was thinking that I could take on the job as Purchasing Manager. I know everything about that job, since I've basically been doing it all along."

"I don't need a Purchasing Manger because I have you as the Purchasing Clerk. You already do everything a manager would do. Why should I give you more money for a job that you already do?"

William understood and was prepared, "Mr. Oakley, have you ever considered expanding the responsibilities of the manager's job? For example, you don't have anyone covering the local sales area. I mean if you need to place an order and you live close by, you have to come to the plant to place your order. There's no one to come by and see if there is anything else they need to complete their project. There isn't a local salesman."

William continued his explanation about how to increase sales while providing the advancement that he needed. Mr. Oakley sat quietly and listened. When William has finished his spiel, he made the following offer.

"You have quite a head on your shoulders for business. I'll tell you what – I'll hire you in this position that you describe and I'll double your salary and give you a commission on your sales. We'll try it for three months. If you can prove to me that this idea is financially beneficial for Lumberton, the position will become permanent." Mr. Oakley had lit a cigar after finishing the bear claws and the order lingered in the air.

Mr. Oakley and William exchanged firm handshakes. As he walked out of the office, he smiled and gave himself an imaginary pat on the back. He had just improved his station in life. A very happy William left the office and began his new position the following Monday.

William fit into the position perfectly. In less than three months, he had built himself a sizeable client list and his commission checks were more than his salary as a clerk. He moved from his mother's house to a small cottage in town. He bought a shiny new ragtop car. He felt invincible. Everything was going his way. Now would be the perfect time to call on Mr. Miller.

The Millers went to the same church as William. The upcoming Sunday there would be an ice cream social after services. That would be a good time to speak to Mr. Miller and let him know that he was coming up in the world. He also looked forward to possibly spending some time with Roseanna.

William stood at the back of the church as the parishioners slowly filed out the door. As Mr. Miller approached, William asked him if he may have a word with him. Mr. Miller smiled and agreed. "Meet me in the garden."

When Roseanna got near, he said hello. "You look lovely today, Miss Roseanna. Yellow is a perfect color for you on such a beautiful spring day."

"Why, thank you Mr. Rivers," she responded.

William found Mr. Miller standing alone with a cup of ice cream in his hand. "Mr. Miller, thank you for talking to me. I wanted to let you know that I have made big improvements in my life since our last talk. I got a promotion at work, moved into my own cottage, bought a car and have accumulated money in my savings account. I feel that I am now in a position to court Roseanna properly. I respectfully ask, again, may I have permission to court your daughter?"

"Roseanna and I have talked of this at length. She is not only agreeable to having you come calling, she wonders why it took you so long to ask me. But, take this as a warning, don't ever take advantage or compromise her in any manner. You may pick her up this evening around 6 p.m." With that Mr. Miller turned and walked away. William was so excited he almost yelled out "HOLY Shit!!" but caught himself just in time.

He pulled up to the Miller's house in his freshly washed and waxed car. The top was up because he didn't know how Roseanna would feel about her long red hair being mussed up by the wind. He had a small bouquet of Primroses. He wanted to keep things simple.

On the way to her house, he stopped and made reservations at the Colonade Restaurant. He was ready.

William rang the doorbell and could see Rosanna skip down the stairs. She was wearing a light blue dress with little pink flowers. Her hair flowed freely in waves around her face. It didn't seem as though she was wearing any make-up except the slight hint of color on her lips. She was more than beautiful; she was perfect in William's eyes.

Rosanna asked if the top of the car could be put down. William complied. As they rode off towards the restaurant, William was beyond happy. He was with the only girl who had ever caught his eye. He had worked hard for the opportunity to get to know her. He would work even harder in the future because he knew, without a doubt, this is the woman he would marry. This is the woman with whom he would spend the rest of his life. Rosanna would be the mother of his children.

William's dream came true. After courting Rosanna for just over a year, they became engaged. William built her a house as a token of proof of his ability to take care of her. Her father approved and they were married. They were blessed with two children, a boy and a girl.

And… they lived happily ever after…

WHAT I LEARNED

- For a period of at least one year after passing, even unpleasant people achieve sainthood.

- If it's too good to be true, it is too good to be true.

- Happiness comes from within you. It is a choice.

- A picture may speak 1,000 words, but not all of them are the truth.

- What I thought was important at age 30 is not the same as what is important to me at age 60.

- I should have spent more time with my parents in their later years.

- A university degree doesn't make you smarter, just more educated in specific subjects.

- Everyone has baggage. Be grateful for what you have both good and bad in your life....one makes you happy and the other really does make you stronger.

- Learn patience early because later on you'll be too busy and too impatient to take the time to learn how to be patient.

- Can't have it all exactly at the time you want. But sometimes you can have a bit of what you want just when you need it the most.

- The minute you park a distance from the store front, a space will open right next to the door.

- If you have any doubts about getting married to a person then don't do it. Wait until there are no doubts. That's why long engagements are a good thing.

- Make saving money a daily habit – the future isn't that far off and every day can turn into a rainy day.

- Not every situation needs a reaction. However, sometimes an honest reaction is better than being silent.

- No matter what your problem is, someone else will have a bigger one.

- Where ever you are, there you are.

- No one person is irreplaceable.

- Running away doesn't work because you always take yourself with you.

- Today is the first day of the rest of your life.

- If you never have bad times you will be unable to recognize and appreciate the good times.

- If I had to do my life over again, I'd probably make better mistakes.

- Where I am today is exactly where I was meant to be.

- Being a jerk isn't always an indication of mental incompetency. Sometimes a jerk is just a jerk.

- What you think of me is none of my business.

- If you're gossiping about me, someone else is being left alone for the moment. Don't worry your turn will come around sooner or later.

- Never date a man who has not experienced the loss of a loved one. He will not know the true value of loving in the here and now.

- Accept who you are because it's too time-consuming to try to be someone you are not.

THIS PAGE INTENTIONALLY LEFT BLANK.

What have you learned?

YOU GOT FAMILY

I was five years old when I started first grade. I was the smallest girl in Mrs. Wightman's class. I don't remember all that much about first grade, but I imagine it was much like all my other grade school years.

Recess was my favorite time of the school day. Hopscotch, swings and monkey bars were my favorite activities in the school yard. A feeling of dread always came over me when we had to choose teams because I was always the last one chosen. I was afraid of catching a ball, so I was not good at softball, kick ball, dodge ball, or anything else that had to do with balls. I was not a fast runner, so any races or activity requiring speed was just not something I would be good or even marginally acceptable at doing. So I was always the last chosen and although my childhood feelings were always hurt, I knew why.

When I got up into the middle school years, I knew that much of the team choosing had to do as much with personality as it did with talent. I wasn't much of a group follower and tended to have one or two friends at a time rather than a whole gaggle. There was a time when it bothered me to not be a part of the "in crowd" and I talked to my mother about it in the presence of my grandmother. I was accepted at Rainbow Girls and no one was ever mean to me, but I was never invited to a party or asked to be a part of a group activity. I had known these girls from first grade on, and yet, most of the time I was treated like an outsider.

My mother responded by telling me that it was OK for me not to be a part of a group because I was too independent to follow the crowd. I had a mind of my own. I walked away thinking that I just would like to go to one of their parties. Just one. Why was I good enough to be nice to in Rainbow, but not good enough to go to one of their social activities?

Grandma pulled me aside and said, "F…ck 'em. Ya don't need 'em anyway. Ya got family." I smiled. It was always a surprise to me when I heard her talk like that. In my mind she was the epitome of moral being. "Live by the golden rule," she would preach but I think she may have meant – if you think someone is going

Grandma Nora Bartee

to treat you badly, make sure to do the same for/to them. I once asked her, what the golden rule really was. "Treat others as you would want to be treated, but if they don't do unto you nice, do unto them first." Oh, Grandma… I loved you so dearly.

The truth of the matter was, that even if I had been invited to go to one of their parties, I probably would not have attended. It made me very nervous to be in large groups of people where I would have to socialize. My mother would plan birthday parties for me and just before the party, I would become very ill. I'd be vomiting and spending time in the bathroom until I would ask my mother to call everyone and cancel. My mother would be disappointed because we would spend hours in the preparation just to have no guests. After a while, we only planned birthday parties that were family oriented except for a very close friend or two.

When I was a teenager, I had a few close friends that my brothers liked. It wasn't much of a surprise that they were willing to take us with them on their Friday or Saturday nights out. My father, in his infinite wisdom thought I (we) were safer if we went out with my brothers and cousins rather than going out on our own. I never quite understood that because with my friends there was always a destination and an activity. But, with the boys, it was just going "out" riding around in the car until we could find something to do. That "something" wasn't usually anything that even resembled good behavior.

One time we stole a flashing yellow "detour" sign and placed it at the head of the bridge leading to Bethel Island. There was only one

way onto the island and one way off. It was a Friday night and weekend visitors who were unfamiliar to the area would turn at the detour sign, drive all the way down the levee road and end right back up at the head of the bridge. We parked our car off to the side and watched as the weekenders drove ring-around-the-rosey. We thought the whole thing was so much fun and we laughed ourselves silly.

Another time, after days of rain, we drove out into a less populated area and pulled up the street signs and relocated them to other corners. So now Maple Street was Green Road and San Joaquin Avenue was now Bridges Lane. We didn't get to witness any confusion, but in our imagination we could see how frustrated some drivers could get if they weren't familiar with the area.

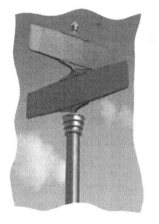

As I see it, being chosen last for teams because I could not throw or catch a ball, nor could I run fast, and was not so very popular, all lead up to my learning to be a part of whatever was going on. I would find a way to fit into whatever or whoever was around as long as the group was very small. Sometimes that wasn't a smart idea and sometimes it was excellent. Mostly, I discovered that I liked the few close friends and felt most comfortable just being with one or two of them at a time. Besides when I was with them I didn't vomit.

SUCH VERY BAD GIRLS

I have no idea why Lena and I clicked as friends. It really doesn't matter why, what matters is that we liked the same things, were goofy and just a bit mischievous. It was nice that she had a swimming pool, but in all the years I knew her, I think I was actually IN that pool only six times. Not much since I knew her from grade school through high school.

Lena was tall with dark hair and I was short with blonde hair. She was musically inclined and I was not so much. We both loved going to the movies, playing board games, watching old movies on TV, swimming in her pool, and aspiring to growing up and living in our very own place with no siblings or parents to tell us what to do. When we were in high school, our boyfriends were next door neighbors and best friends. That was convenient.

I liked going to Lena's house because her parents didn't mind if she wandered the streets of Brentwood without supervision. My parents, on the other hand, would never have allowed me to just go without an agenda anywhere in town. In my mind, I rationalized that if I got permission to go spend time at Lena's house, it was permission to do whatever Lena's parents would allow Lena to do.

Lena and I like to build houses from refrigerator boxes. We would go to the local appliance store over on First Street and ask if there were any empty boxes that we could have. There almost always were two of the large boxes ready for us to take away. We dropped them over our heads and toted them back to Lena's house. It was nearly a straight shot from the store to Lena's – only about four blocks. But, it was slow going because we had to lift the boxes to check for traffic and other obstacles. Once the boxes were in Lena's

135

back yard, we drew flowers, cut out windows and imagined them as our own homes. It was a wonderful way to spend the day.

Spending the night was just as much fun. In the summer time we would climb over her back fence. I have no clue why we did that because we could have just as easily gone out the gate. But, anyway… it would be about 9 P.M. and the streets didn't have a lot of traffic. Brentwood was a very small town and about the only "action" was to be found in one of, maybe, three drinking establishments for the adults. For the kids, Delta Theatre held the most opportunity for fun in the afternoons and evenings.

Lena and I didn't go to the theatre. That would have been far too easy to get permission. We wanted to do something that we didn't want to get caught doing. I suppose it was the wild streak in us. So… we walked around looking in the store windows and avoiding anyone who might tell our parents that we were out. It was a game. A hide-and-seek kind of game.

During those years, Brentwood had a beat cop. He actually walked the streets with a baton looking for activity of an unlawful nature. He would grab the juvenile delinquents by the collar, call their parents and issue some type of punishment. These were the kids who shoplifted and caused mischief that would actually hurt people. We never hurt anyone. We never stole anything. We had no objective except to not get caught for being out wandering the streets after dark without a destination or purpose.

I don't remember the name of the beat cop, but for this story we will call him Officer Doright. I'm sure there must have been more than one Officer Doright. It's a nice name so that's who he will be.

Officer Doright, as Lena and learned from observation walked in a square around the blocks on one side of Oak Street and then walked the other side. He was methodical. We were twelve and if we could figure it out, we were certain a real crook could figure it out and easily avoid observation.

We usually walked around town until we found Officer Doright and then politely wished him a good evening. We would inform him that we were on our way to Lena's house and hoped he had an uneventful evening. He was good with that after quizzing us about where we had been and why were we out so late. He would ask us questions about the movie that was currently playing to test to see if we really were coming from the Delta Theatre. Sometimes he would ask us what the special was at the Creamery or whatever restaurant we may have told him we had been visiting. The trick was to know the answers to the questions and not get caught by lack of information. So we would go into the restaurant the check out what was going on and same thing for the movies. We had our finger on the pulse of Brentwood without ever really participating in anything.

One night we had managed to stay out until almost midnight. We had greeted Officer Doright several hours prior. We turned the corner at the Bank of America and practically ran right into the good officer.

"Girls. Didn't I just talk to you in front of the library?" He asked. "Yes. I believe that was you right there in front of the library. It must have been you because I don't see many tall & short girl combos your age roaming around in the evening." He looked us square in the eyes – well – he looked Lena square in the eyes because she was closer to his height than I was. To top it off, I was probably looking at the pavement and praying that he did not call my parents. Officer Doright asked Lena, "You do know that your house is in the opposite direction, don't you?" Then he turned his attention to me, "Linda, I know that if your parents knew you were out here, it would be a month of Sundays until you got too see the likes of the sidewalks of Brentwood again." I looked up with pleading eyes to not call them but there was no sound coming from my mouth. We were caught. We lost the game that night.

Officer Doright walked with us back to Lena's house and watched us go in the gate. He did not ring the doorbell or call my parents. He simply saw us safely home. There would be no grounding or restrictions from visiting each other. We were grateful.

Unfortunately, our gratitude did not stay ingrained in our heads. We knew that we would have to be very careful from here on out because Officer Doright might not be so merciful if he were faced with the same decision again. I'm sure the officer thought we had learned a lesson. We did in fact learn a valuable lesson. The lesson we learned was to carry with us a large compact so we can see around the corners of the buildings.

Bank of America Building

EAT YOUR WORDS

Sometimes I don't know why I say the things that I do. That was especially true as a young girl in my early teens. Further complicating things was the type of day that I had. If things went well and I was praised or complemented, my head would swell and I'd think that I was invincible. Thoughts that anyone would say or do anything that could knock me off my own self-imposed pedestal just could not be imagined. I wasn't always confident or self-assured. In fact I was seldom of that mind set. But, when I was, I mean I really was.

It was one of those nights when there was no more room at the table. We were shoulder to shoulder and plate to plate. Mom had made her family favorite Goulash, green salad, biscuits, and ice tea. There would be pie for dessert. Yummmm.... And everyone wants some.

It was summer and the boys/men were still wearing their grubby, dirty work clothes. Even after scrubbing their hands and face, they still smelled of motor oil, creosote and just plain old dirt. I didn't mind. In fact I barely noticed the yuckyness of them anymore. But, it always seemed to me that the dirtier they were, the hungrier they were. That made perfect sense to me. The harder they worked, the dirtier they would be, and in turn, the harder they worked the more food needed to fill up those hunger holes.

We were settling in. Food was being passed around the table. The real conversation had not yet started, but I knew it was about to happen any second now. Just about as I was wondering what the guys had really done that day, my little brother literally threw a biscuit over to my littlest brother – which he caught in mid-flight. Just as the biscuit was flying through the air, there could be heard – ohs; ahhhs;

no's – coming out of the mouths of various diners. Then they all looked over at my father, waiting.

Now, we may have looked like a tribe of dirty curmudgeons sitting around a feasting table, but ill-manners were always unacceptable. It was always "Please pass the…" and "May I have…" and chewing with your mouth closed, and all those other things that make eating in a group more pleasant. Throwing food across the table was definitely not on the list of acceptable behavior no matter how perfect the toss or catch.

My father, flabbergasted at the sight of the biscuit landing in my brother's hand, quickly said "Whaaaat? This is not a ball field! Gimme those biscuits!" indicating that neither boy would be enjoying that sauce by soaking up a bit of enjoyment. As he took the biscuits in his hand, he said "We're not heathens here."

Somewhere, from a place at the table came a sound that went something like this "Not today, but maybe tomorrow." It was a small voice, said under the breath and probably not meant for anyone else to hear. I looked up and everyone was looking at me. And then it hit me – I was the one who said it. Those words came from my mouth, my vocal chords. . It was too late to grab the words, still hanging in a bubble over my head, and gobble them up unnoticed.

Silence. I heard silence – except the voice of my father, yelling at me. "What did you say? You think this is funny? You can take your plate and leave the table. Go eat on the mantle." His demand was not to be dismissed. I took my plate, utensils and iced tea. I placed my things on the mantel and tears flowed down my face as I tried to eat my dinner. I was just a short girl and I barely reached the mantle.

I no sooner started eating when the silence ended and I could hear the conversation from the kitchen. Everyone was rolling in laughter. I imagined them all on the floor, between the chairs and under the table because they could not contain their snickers. So, I wondered why I was being punished.

Oh yeah… now I remember… it's not OK to be funny if it is coupled with disrespect. Well… I won't make that mistake again. I'll either be funny OR I'll be disrespectful… well maybe I should just take disrespectful off the table – literally.

THIS PAGE INTENTIONALLY LEFT BLANK.

Creative Cub Scouting

When I first contacted the 1-800 for the Boy Scouts of America, I simply wanted for my son to be able to be a part of a Cub Scout Troop. It was just a simple phone call to ask how I could make that happen. But, before the call was over, I was a Den Mother of a troop of six boys. OK. So how hard could it be? My mother had been a Den Mother and she didn't find it to be an unreasonable time expense. She loved all those little boys who sent her homemade cards of well wishes. If she could do it then so could I.

I went to visit another troop to see how things were done. I had a meeting with a few people and then they gave me a list of boys' names. I was to choose the day and time. Fortunately, I wasn't working at the time and school was in session – so I picked a day after school. And the meetings began.

All those little boys were adorable. Sweet faces and eager to please attitudes. I was determined to have the best Cub Scouts in the area. My boys would earn their badges quickly. I knew I could make this *soooo* much fun. Making it fun didn't necessarily mean following all those long steps that were "suggested" in the Den Mother's Handbook. My idea was to just plan fun things for us and then figure out which badge would fit the activity.

Our first adventure was a field trip to the local dairy. They learned about the cows and each got to experience how to milk them. They learned what happens to the milk after it leaves the cow. There was hay pitching and cow pie clean up. The boys were laughing and listening to the dairyman. I was impressed with how well behaved they were. When we got back home, I gave them a little test to see how much they learned. I looked on the chart, hmmm, ANIMAL HUSBANDRY gets check off.

I had a little fire in our house and the living and dining room walls needed to be re-painted. There must be a badge for that, so the boys all grabbed a paint roller and painted as high as their little arms could reach. Wow! More than half the task had been accomplished! HOME REPAIRS and PAINTING Badge checked off!

They earned the LANDSCAPE ARCHITECTURE Badge when I had them pull the weeds around my flower beds and haul the trash out to the street. These kids are coming in handy!

We went for a walk through the woods at the end of our street and I decided that was worth a PHYSICAL FITNESS Badge. And we tried to identify plants and trees so that would also encompass the NATURE Badge.

One night I had them help me prepare dinner and dessert. They all left with cookies and recipes. Great! I get help with dinner and they earn a COOKING Badge.

I thought I was doing great! I thought the boys were having a wonderful time and they were earning badges!

I had them write about their family life and had them take their work back to their parents. Yeah! JOURNALISM Badge! But that one wasn't met with a round of approval by the families. I told the boys to put down their innermost feelings and some of the parents didn't like reading what was in the folder.

Eventually, my Cub Scout leadership abilities came into question. The people who had given me the go-ahead to become a Den Mother were calling me on the carpet. Had I been using the assigned worksheet for each badge? Who could verify that they had actually completed the tasks for the badge properly? Well... No, I hadn't been using the worksheet and I wasn't sure how there could be any "witnesses" to what they had done. Were the boys not enjoying their time with me? Were any of them saying I was abusing them?

That wasn't the point, I was told. Of course the boys loved their den meeting times. But, it appeared they were more of "handy boys" than den members. The boys needed to earn their badges in the manner of steps set out by the Scout Council. I said something like, that would take forever and the boys were just little boys who needed more timely acknowledge of what they accomplished.

Needless to say, I wasn't a very good Den Mother in the eyes of Boy Scouts of America. I was stripped of my uniform and my son and the other boys were put into a more "appropriate" den. This Den Mother lived right down the street and her son was a good friend of my son. She always played exactly by the rules – no creatively rearranging the requirements.

I understood and didn't put up a fuss. After all, when being a part of a big organization like that, rules are important. I wasn't exactly a rule-abider. But it was interesting that the boys had to walk past my house to get to the new Den Mother's and they always seemed to be stopping in to see me. They would come to play with my son, but sit with me for cookies and milk. Many of them joined us on some of our family excursions. It was better that way because I didn't have to figure out which badge they could earn for whatever activity.

I love the Boy Scout Organization; it provides structure and a sense of belonging. But the free-spirit in me thinks there is just as much importance in finding one's own way through the interest of the moment. Every experience is badge-worthy.

So far this month, I've earned about 17 self-created imaginary badges.

THIS PAGE INTENTIONALLY LEFT BLANK.

You can write your own memory of something creative you've accomplished or, maybe, something you accomplished even if it wasn't so creative.

Move It or Else

In 1953 Morris and Lois moved into their home on Sycamore Avenue in Brentwood, California. Morris and his brothers did most of the work themselves and hired out the things that they couldn't do themselves. When the kitchen was framed out, dry-walled and ready for the cabinet installation, Morris took the task on himself. He made the cabinets and installed them at just about waist high. When he completed his handiwork, he brought in Lois to present to her the brand new kitchen.

Lois looked around the kitchen with tears in her eyes. This kitchen was perfect. Well... except for one little teeny tiny thing. Morris was 6'2" tall and Lois was 5'2" tall and that means that the cabinets were waist-high on Morris but almost armpit height for Lois. It was immediately obvious that the kitchen cabinets would have to be removed and re-installed. Within just a few days, the kitchen was Lois' height proportionate and it truly was perfect.

The couple loved their new home which was set on an acre of apricot orchard land. Over the years the orchard provided many canned apricots, apricot pies, apricot jam, dried apricots and pick-em-off-the-tree and eat em goodness. But after a decade the trees began to die off leaving open land around the home. Because of the available space, family members began working on their vehicles and/or storing various things on the land.

When Morris died, Lois wanted to clean up the property and possibly implement some other money making ideas concerning the space. She had to figure out how to get the stored vehicles off the land to free up the space.

She called every family member and told them that she needed to get the cars removed. Lois often had a bark that was far worse than her bite and many times her threats were empty. She would rant and rave and when it was over, she'd go on as though she had never been upset. That is – until the next time she would get riled up over whatever the issue was. During this time the issue was the cars on the property.

She made more phone calls and a few of the cars disappeared by virtue of the owners taking action. Things would calm down when she saw "something" was being done. Then, a few months later, the phones calls would begin again. In the last phone call, she was very specific. Move your cars or she would have them towed. A car would be gone here or there as a result, but there were still too many.

Lois loved family gatherings and she decided it was time for another one. It was Labor Day and a good excuse for a pot-luck barbecue. She cooked and planned and prepared for the large crowd. People began arriving early to help with the preparations.

As the family arrived they found a beautifully cleared property free of cars, equipment, lawn mowers, bicycles, etc. "Hey! What happened to my car? Where's my welding machine?" was the outcry from several attendees. Lois responded with "You mean those things that you hadn't touched in three years? The ones that hadn't run in just as long? Those things are gone. They were taken by the man I hired to clear the yard. A towing company gave me a little cash for those rusty old cars. That's what's paying for this little shin-dig today. Money well spent, I'd say."

No one argued with her. There were a few grumbles but for the most part everyone stayed silent. The group enjoyed the steaks, ribs, soft drinks, etc. No one questioned Lois. But, that's how it was with

Lois. You don't question or argue with her because one way or another she would ALWAYS win. It might take her a while, but in the end she got what she wanted.

No one ever stored another thing on that property again.

THIS PAGE INTENTIONALLY LEFT BLANK.

When was the last time you stood your ground?

VALUE OF A DOLLAR

At the end of the Civil War, people were still in possession of confederate money. It wasn't worth anything so it could not be used as legal tender to purchase anything. But people held onto the money in hopes that someday, just maybe, it might have some value.

Just before the end of the Civil War, the Welch family moved from Georgia to Texas. Nora was just a young girl, under the age of 16. Before the move, bundles of confederate money were sewn into her petticoat. It was the money the family had saved to set themselves up in their new state of Texas. If their wagon were stopped, the parents believed the young girl would not be searched and the money would be safe. As it turned out, the family was never stopped and the trip was uneventful.

While they made their trek, the Civil War ended. The money in the petticoat would be useless. But, they had union money hidden in other areas of the wagon so they still had enough to get them started. Nora was told she could keep the confederate money. She wasn't convinced that the money would never again have any value, so she held onto it.

Years passed and she still had the money. When her children were born and grew into toddlers, she gave them the money to play with. They had a great time with it and most of it ended up torn, battered and abused.

One day her husband told her to gather up the money so he could take it to town. A newspaper article said the money could be redeemed for regular money. The value would be pennies on the dollar, but still it was money that could be spent. Nora looked around the room and saw bits and pieces of the money scattered around the room. She handed the few whole bills she could gather over to her husband. Out of the hundreds of bills, she now only had less than a dozen.

The couple looked at each other and were disappointed that the amount they would receive would hardly make it worth the long trip into town. But the money had a different value. They thought of the fun the children had playing with the money. They thought of the giggles and laughter and realized that the money had a value that could not be equated with any amount on the dollar. The bills bought hours of entertainment to their children which made the money priceless.

THEN THERE WERE BOYS

There's something about going from first grade through high school in the same school system, in the same small town, with the same kids. By the time your teenage years hit and an interest develops in the opposite sex, the potential candidates for romance are boys or girls that you've seen grow through missing teeth, unruly hair, and awkward gawky years and then emerge in to beautiful young people. The girls are suddenly blessed with beautiful complexions and flowing long hair. The boys become handsome young men with flashy smiles, muscles and perfectly groomed hair. It is a true caterpillar-like metamorphosis.

Eighth grade was the start of most of the kids' introduction into male/female socially interactive relationships. There were school dances, church functions, and private parties that begged for attendance. I went to the eighth grade graduation school dance. It was my first dance and I went with a group of girlfriends. We sat at our table and talked about everyone there – who was with whom and who wanted to be with whom.

I had a secret crush on a boy named William. It was his first year in our school system. Oh, I believed he was so very fine, but everyone knew that his heart was with Maria. He was handsome and she was beautiful. Together they just fit. That didn't stop me from crushing and dreaming that he would notice me.

He was walking my way… he stopped at our table… and… he reached out to me and asked me to dance. I simply wanted to say "Yes" but I think it came out as "uhh… yea… uh huh…" I don't think it made any sense, but I was up on my feet and in his arms faster than he could have a chance to change his mind. I looked around hoping that EVERYONE could see that I was dancing with William! But… I noticed that he had this little, kinda, strange, smell when he breathed. OH NO! My heart throb had bad breath. I didn't breath in when my nose was pointed towards his face.

Suddenly he stopped dancing in the middle of the song… "Linda, there's Maria. I want to go dance with her." And he left me. There I was standing in the middle of the dance floor while he ran over to Maria. Where I had hoped everyone had been watching before, I now prayed that no one noticed that he had abandoned me.

It was my first dance with my first dance partner and he left me stranded for another girl. I wondered if it was an indication of how the rest of my life would be. Of course not, I thought.

By the time I got into high school, I had decided that I would not date boys that I had grown up with. I didn't care how dramatic the metamorphosis had been, I still saw them as the little boys who teased me, pulled my hair, and stole my lunch. I was not interested.

That meant that my romantic pool was from boys who transferred into my school or boys from neighboring towns. When I was in, I believe, it was tenth grade. A new boy came to school and he was exactly what I thought I wanted in a boyfriend. We quickly made friends and spent a lot of time talking, probably when we should have been studying. His locker was just one over from mine, so we saw each other often during the day. He never made any advances towards me that would ever lead me to believe he thought of me as potential girlfriend material. But we were friends.

One day, he asked if he could walk me home from school. I was delighted. Of course he could. My mind was going crazy – was this the next step in becoming closer? I couldn't think of any reason other than that from him wanting to walk me home. We met up at the edge of the parking lot and started my usual walk toward my house. It wasn't far, only about 20 minutes if you focused on walking. I was determined to drag it out to an hour.

As we walked, we pasted the houses on my street and he asked me who lived in each one. When we were almost to my house he asked, "Do you mind if I ask you something about the family that lives up the street?"

"You mean the Sullivan's? Sure, go ahead, I've know them almost my whole life." I responded.

"I really like Margie and would like to take her out. Do you think I should ask her father for permission? I know her family is old fashioned like that. What do you think I should do?"

WHAT!!! This was Maria all over again!! In my mind, I was thinking... why would he want to date her when he could have all this – ME! We were already friends. What could he possibly see in her? She wasn't even that pretty. Sure she was friendly and had a good personality, but I knew her growing up and I knew some skeletons in her closet. She and I had not been friendly for many years. In fact, I often avoided her.

"Well... Sam... Your right, her father is very old fashioned and would probably appreciate your asking him if it's all right for you to date Margie. Bye." I ran up my driveway, went straight to my room and covered my pillow in tears. I thought to myself – it's OK, it will never last. There's still a chance for me because we are still friends.

Margie and Sam dated throughout high school and college. They got married, moved back to Brentwood and are still married more than 40 years later.

But, there could still be a chance for me. I just know that any day now, he'll come to his senses and realize that he should have dated me instead. So what if we haven't spoken since high school? So what if I'm more than 3,000 miles away? Then again – I still think Bruce Willis is waiting for me to be available. I visit reality only on selected days.

THIS PAGE INTENTIONALLY LEFT BLANK.

This reminder of innocence in young like must remind you of something about your youth. You can write your notes about it here.

AIN'T NO RIZZO

A teenager's reputation in high school can make or break the enjoyment of the whole high school experience. I enjoyed a good reputation for the first two years of high school. My third year wasn't so great. But before that, I was always seen as the "little nice girl". I was very small compared to my peers and somehow that equated to needing to be "a bit of a baby" in the eyes of most. As people got to know me, they realized that I was not a baby, but still a nice girl.

Over the summer of my second and third year of high school, I met a boy. (Trouble always seems to start with those words – I met a boy.) He was the brother of a girl my older brother was dating. I thought he was very handsome and fun – I was smitten. We spent some time making out with it always ending with him pushing me to go further and further. I wasn't ready for that. He showered me with flattery and telling me he thought I was special. But the summer ended, as all summers do, and I figured that was just it – done, over.

School started and I was happy to see everybody although I was nervous at the same time. I had a lot of social catching up to do since I was never a part of the "crowd" that hung out together in the summertime. I was always just on the edge, liked but not included. I never felt hurt or bullied or anything of those things. I just accepted it and convinced myself that I was just fine without the parties and group functions. I had my select friends and summer was always filled with laughter, family visits and new adventures. In fact, those cliques had no idea how much fun I was having and what they were missing by not including me.

The boys at school never had much to do with me. A couple of them were really good friends and we talked only during school. The others were usually polite and respectful, but they seldom had much to say to me except during class and while working on class assignments. A few of the more popular boys would say hello and actually use my name – "Hey Linda! What's new?" or "Good Morning, Linda, nice day, huh?"

By the start of school that year, I had blossomed into a busty young lady. I hated having such big boobs because now they seemed to be the only thing the boys noticed about me. Some were cruel by making comments about how I got to be so large. Others would cat-call followed by some crude remark. The ones who used to use my name still did just that, but the eyes were no longer on my face. Already the year was not off to a good start. Then, things got worse.

My summer boyfriend had transferred to my school. When I first saw him, I thought "This is great! I'll have someone to walk me to classes and hold my hand." I thought this was really going to be a good thing. Unfortunately, I couldn't have been more wrong. Summer Boyfriend wouldn't even speak to me. If I approached him he would literally RUN the other direction. I was devastated.

I was walking through the corridors, as I did every morning. The boys were sitting on the half-wall that separated the corridor from the parking lot. That's when they would usually tell me good morning or make some off-color remark. This morning was the worst morning in my life when I heard "Hey Linda – Summer Boyfriend wants to suck your tits, he says to meet him at his car!" Then another yelled "Yeah! He wants to poke you again!"

I didn't know the names of the boys who were yelling at me. They weren't the ones I had gone to school with my whole life. They weren't the ones who usually told me good morning. I surmised they would be the ones most likely to cut school, meet in the park and smoke cigarettes while planning a means to being thrown in juvenile hall. They were the rowdy boys, the bad boys. It didn't matter because the boys I liked were in earshot and they all heard. I ran as fast as I could to the safety of my next class.

I didn't know what to do so I ignored them. Or at least, I didn't let them know that they upset me. I was livid with Summertime Boyfriend! How dare him to tell these awful boys such horrible things about me. I had no way of proving that they were either liars or were misinformed. I managed to corner Summer Boyfriend and give him a piece of my mind. He said nothing. He just turned and ran away.

I stopped walking through the corridor to class. Instead I took the long way around that avoided the boys sitting on the wall. When I did see one of the dreaded yelling boys, he or they said nothing to me. I was as though it was forgotten and they had moved on to harassing someone else. I felt sorry for their next victim whoever she was.

Years later, Summer Boyfriend and I met again. It was an on-line encounter which I could have ignored. But, the years have turned me into a strong confident and somewhat aggressive woman. I wrote him an e-mail and let him know just how his lies had hurt me way back then. I explained that it changed the way I viewed potential boyfriends after that. I lost my ability to trust male counterparts and that mistrust continued into my adult years. I told him he should be thankful that my brother and cousins didn't find out what he had done because their retribution would have been significant.

I didn't expect a response so I was surprised when he wrote back. He apologized in a way that I knew he meant it from his heart. His only excuse was that he was a disrespectful, cowardly boy who clearly earned a sound thumping by my brother and cousins. He said he had been warned not to mess around with me because the Bartee Boys were very protective and took care of problems in their own way. He also told me that he knew that I would be disappointed with him as a boyfriend because he was one of those guys who eventually hurt me far more than he actually did. I was someone who never cut a class or drank a beer or smoked anything. I would not be found out drag racing or shoplifting. I would never have survived in his world and he would never have fit into mine.

As we continued writing, I realized that he had grown into a responsible, caring man. I appreciated the apology and was glad we had a chance to clear the air. I found out that he had three young sons who were close to adulthood. I asked if would be telling our story to them to prevent them from breaking some young girl's heart. He said that he has told them stories of how much trouble he got into and hoped they could learn from his mistakes. So far, he said, none had been to juvey and they were all planning on going to college. He considered that to be a step in the right direction.

Summer Boyfriend and I have some similarities as Sandy Olsen and Danny Zucko from the movie *Grease*. But, I'm no Sandy and he was certainly no Danny. Then again, he tried to make me out as being Rizzo, but I wasn't her either. In the end, I was just a young girl smitten by a boy's charm and looks. I hope I never make that mistake again.

PRETTY BOY BILL

His name was Bill and he was handsome... so very handsome and I was so very surprised when he asked me out for a second, and then a third and fourth date. Then I realized that we were, in fact, dating that lead to a true relationship within a couple of months. I had a key to his place and he had a key to mine. We each had toothbrushes resting in the medicine cabinet of both residences.

He travelled a lot. During those times we talked on the phone almost nightly. Before long, I was sure that I was in love. I thought things were going well. He had met my son and spent holidays at my family gatherings. Everyone loved him.

We went to the car races, theater, 4-star restaurants, he accompanied me to corporate functions, we took walks, went swimming, and rented movies. We cooked together and shopped together. We always had fun no matter what we did.

Imagine my surprise when, after a business trip, he announces, "I can't do this anymore. Please gather up your things and leave." I didn't know what was wrong. I thought maybe we could talk it out, but he didn't want to talk. He just wanted me gone. That was difficult because my son had dropped me off at his house and planned on picking me up two days later. Bill did not offer to take me home. It was too soon for me to call my son to come get me – we didn't have cell phones. I started walking without being really sure of where I was going.

Before too long, maybe a few blocks, Bill pulled up beside me and asked me to get in. I did as he asked and we drove in silence for the twenty miles back to my home. I quietly said "thank you" and left the car as quickly as I could to the safety of my own space. Then I went directly to the closet and bathroom to gather his things. They looked like two trash bags ready to go to the dump.

I didn't hear from him again for weeks. When he did finally call, it was to ask me if I could help him with some sewing. I told him I was too busy, but what I really wanted to say was that whatever I did that made him break up with me, I was sorry. It took everything inside me to not apologize for his rudeness.

Bill did call again. We did talk again. But, it was never about us breaking up. It was always about what was happening in his life. He hated his job. He missed his old girlfriend (the one he left behind in Florida – not me). He discovered he had a teen-age daughter. It seemed I was always picking him up, dusting him off, and being his friend.

That's what we were – friends. Well, let's just say, he assumed we were close friends and I was guarded but friendly.

Our friendship lasted for years. As he moved around the country, there were telephone calls at all hours of the night and day. Every time he would meet a new woman, he would call and tell me all about her. I listened and advised him to be honest and open and to not fall too quickly. But, he didn't listen and all the new women ended up much the same way our relationship had ended. Although all the break-ups were of his choosing, each one left him with a sense of failure and lowered his self-esteem.

This man was handsome, financially privileged, and professionally successful, and yet he doubted himself and questioned all his emotions with every relationship. I didn't understand why I was always the one he turned to for "counseling." But, somehow I had fallen into that role.

I believe that relationships are not truly over until both parties can say it is over. For me, I finally saw my relationship with Bill for exactly what it was – a one-sided friendship. It was time to clear the air and when I told him I never wanted to hear from him again, I felt a since of freedom. I never tried to resume the friendship. It was over and I knew that this time, it was truly over for him as well.

The relationship/friendship with Bill was a learning experience. I no longer put blinders on because a man is seriously handsome and can afford to take me places. I realize now that the reason why we got on so well at first was because I was a good listener. Our first dates were full of the red flags that I ignored. Conversations were always about him, his exes, his family, his, his, his. I was so busy looking at the face, that I wasn't paying attention.

Last I heard, he was in a very long term relationship and I know nothing more about what happened to him. I only hope he is happy and has learned to not be so self-focused, but rather emotionally available to the new woman in his life.

THIS PAGE INTENTIONALLY LEFT BLANK.

You don't have to be in your youth to learn hard lessons in matters of the heart.

I HEART YOU

I always seem to struggle through the month of February. In my mind it's a small month that is packed with stuff – National Freedom Day, Groundhog Day, Rosa Parks Day, National Wear Red Day, Lincoln's Birthday, Susan B Anthony Birthday, President's Day, and let's add Arkansas' Daisy Gatson Bates Day. In spite of all the listed holidays, February is still known to be the month of love. Valentine's Day seems to over-shadow all the others.

My struggle with this month of love is that I am a romantic disguised as a cynic. I make jokes about the best thing about Valentine's Day is the day after when the candy can be bought at 75% off. I send funny cards and reserve all my goosheyness for my great-grandbabies who love getting my little gifts declaring my love for them. If you pull back the mask and look underneath you will find that I'm not just a romantic, I am utterly and completely hopeless. I am also a realist. I suppose that means I'm a realistic hopeless romantic with a few issues.

I was watching a television program about a wedding. It was beautiful. The gown was incredible with bits of shiny beads, pearls and lace. It fit her like a glove and her beautiful figure was easily recognized. Flowers were everywhere and all the guests were both smiling and crying. It would surely be a day the couple would remember for the rest of their lives.

At a friend's wedding, I watched and listened. I noticed that somewhere inside me I experienced a bit of stinging when the vows were said and done and the minister pronounced them "husband and wife." It was like the words were said in slow motion – h u s b a n d and   w i f e. That part is always saved to the end of the ceremony, like they don't tell you the punch line of the joke until the end. Husband and Wife. As if their names were no longer John and Mary, but rather "husband and wife." I turned off the television and decided to put it out of my mind by baking some bread. I like to bake as a distraction from things that are disturbing.

The baking didn't help because I kept thinking that I didn't really know what all that meant – or maybe I did know what it meant and was uncomfortable with it. I'm sure it's the later of the two. I am a wife and I have a husband. It's a path I chose many years ago – more than 40 in fact. It was a decision I made with open eyes. As is the case with most newlyweds, I was young and inexperienced. When I think about it now I don't understand how young couples can be expected to make life-altering decisions at such a delicate, tender, age. It's like saying at age 15, I'm gonna love roses my entire life and then realizing when you're 40, that you like hydrangeas better. I suppose that's why divorce was invented.

Strangely, I've never been a wife to a man that I felt I could have spent my entire life with. I've been married to an abuser (Peter) and to a drunk (Mike). If I have to measure, I have far more affection for Mike than I ever had for Peter which is understandable with all things considered. I am now, and have been almost forever, Mike's wife. That means I do wifely things especially now that he is no longer able to take care of himself. I cook, clean, organize, manage, and take care of him because he cannot do these things for himself. Sometimes I do a better job than others, but I always do something for him on a daily basis. He is my husband and that means he is my responsibility.

I could have chosen to get a divorce when I realized that taking the vows meant I would be forever tied to this other person. But, I didn't. I'm a hopeless romantic. No matter how bad things got, I stayed the hopeless romantic. I believed he would leave his mistress, Ms Vodie Aristocrat, and return to me with a renewed vigor towards saving our marriage. That did not happen. When the mistress left him behind, she left a broken man who was not recognizable as the man with whom I had taken my vows.

People ask me how we have been able to stay together so long. They say we must have a secret to making our marriage work. I want to scream out that the only person the marriage works for is Mike. The secret for couples to have a long marriage is to marry someone who will feel a sense of responsibility and will not leave when things are unbearable. And if you split up, make sure you maintain some semblance of a bond, so the healthy one will come to the aid of the unhealthy one during bad times. My advice is to forget love and marry for loyalty. Did I mention that I'm a cynic?

I have a love-hate relationship with Valentine's Day. I'm jealous of the people who I believe have found that true and everlasting love that will sustain them for their entire life, yet I'm happy for them. I long to have had that with the man that I believed would be a true and loving husband. I realize that will never happen. I fantasize that there is still hope for me. I believe that I have little time or energy left to really search for him. I refute the idea that a Prince Charming will ride up and save me from the beast. I would probably tell the prince to ride on and go save his own self anyway. I know that I want true love. I doubt that it will come to me in this lifetime.

Maybe there should be two types of marriages. First there should be the young love marriage that allows for the procreation of our species. If it lasts forever, that's great. The second type of marriage is one based on practicalities like common interests, friendships, sexual compatibility and has nothing to do with producing offspring. This second type of marriage would happen at a later age when each individual has already been through the first type of marriage. Each individual would know themselves as their own person and would be better able to communicate wants, needs, desires, dreams, etc. In fact, the second type of marriage doesn't even have to be a licensed marriage. It could be just two people who join together with a common goal. They don't even have to live in the same house or sleep in the same bed. They just have to be able to depend on getting support, consideration and understanding from each other.

In my opinion, the chances of having a "first type" marriage that lasts till death do part is rare. No one is the same at age 60 as they are at age 20. If what you're looking for is a "death do part" marriage, don't get married until you're already in your 50's. It's easier to keep the romance alive over a period of 20 or 30 years than it is 50 or 60 years.

I think one of my fears of re-marriage is that I'd get sick and my new husband would feel obligated to take care of me. On the other hand, he would get sick and I'd be taking care of him. I've had enough caretaking to last me two more lifetimes. If I get sick – just put me in a nursing home somewhere and visit me on Sundays. I'm afraid he would not do that just as I doubt I would be able to put him in a home.

This year on Valentine's Day I did my usual cynical stuff. I laughed and carried on. Inside I was conflicted. Maybe just staying in bed under the covers for the entire month would have been a better way to handle things. Oh no... wait... I just realized that June will be upon is in no time. June is the wedding month... here I go again.

RUNNING AWAY...

I was probably about 8 years old when I had a confrontation with my mother. I wanted to do something and she didn't want me to do it. So I told her I was going to run away from home.

OK, my mother responded. She was so calm. I don't think she missed a stitch on whatever garment she was mending. Just a very simple "OK". I was indignant. How dare she not take my threat seriously! After all, I was the only girl in this family and I should be treated with far more respect than just an "OK". *Humpf!!!* I'll show her! She's really gonna miss me when I'm gone.

I tromped off to my room, grabbed my little bag and starting packing chosen items of clothing. I didn't have a plan. I didn't know where I would go. But, I knew I wasn't staying here. Pajamas, toothbrush, underwear, a couple of tops and some pants plus my hairbrush – that should do it. I grabbed my pillow and a blanket on my way out.

Passing thru the kitchen to get to the backdoor, I saw Mom was cooking vegetable soup from her garden harvest. I saw the unhusked corn on counter and the ingredients for biscuits. She had already made a peach pie from the orchard's peach trees next door. This would be an incredible dinner and I considered waiting until afterwards to run away. But, I was still angry and decided I needed to make a point.

It was summer, but the day was not so hot that you couldn't breathe. I stood at the end of the drive and thought about what direction would be best. I wondered if the Harrison's had returned

169

from vacation. If not, their outdoor screen room would be a good place to sleep tonight. It was safely tucked behind their big two-story Tudor home. I decided to take a chance and go that direction.

When I approached the house, I could tell I was in luck. No one was around. The family had lots of kids – at least as many as was living at my house – and none of them were outside throwing balls or working in the yard. I went up and rang the doorbell just to be sure. If someone answered I would ask if one of the kids wanted to play. If no one answered, I'd continue on to the back yard and the screen room. No one came to the door.

"Screen Room" – that's what they called it. It was a huge room with ten picnic tables and coordinating benches lined up all in a row. Along the one outside wall was a counter similar to what you would find in a kitchen. The counter was broken in the middle by a giant sized riverstone fireplace. The fireplace had a grill on one end with a spit that was lowered and raised with a round pulley device. There were cabinets with locks and a locked refrigerator. I had been to many cook-outs here and the screen room was always the center of attention because that's where all the food was cooked and consumed. It was a truly wonderful room and I wished my parents would see the logic in having one at our house.

Hmmm… "our house"… I wondered what was going on. It was always my job to set the dinner table and make the salad. We had salad every single night. My father was determined to make me a "Salad Master Chef." He always told me to use my imagination and I tried various spices and condiments, but always said I needed to dig deeper. Each and every salad was praised, but I knew he expected more. I had no idea what he meant, but I kept on trying. Well! I wonder who would make the salad tonight!

I sat in the screen house with my arms crossed and resting on the top of the picnic table and my head resting on my arms. I thought that if I were home I would probably be on my bed reading a book or drawing a picture. I had forgotten to bring the book that was currently holding my attention. I didn't bring a clock so I didn't even know what time it was. I figured at least two hours had gone by. They must be starting to miss me by now.

Somewhere in the back of my mind, I imagined that someone would come looking for me. Someone must surely want me to come home. Then the tears started. Why didn't my mother stop me from leaving? She just let me walk out the door and never even said "Good-Bye". Maybe she didn't love me at all. Maybe she wanted me to run away. Those thought didn't make me mad, they just made me cry harder.

I hadn't quiet finished with my pity-party when I saw Richard walk up from the driveway towards the Screen Room. When he saw me he stopped and asked, "What are you doing here? You should not be here because they are not home."

My hands on my hips, I replied with "Well... What are YOU doing here?" while using my best Little Miss Smarty Pants projection. "They asked me to take care of the dog and cats," he said. He continued with, "You better come on home with me. Mom is about to put dinner on the table."

Sitting in the Screen Room, I waited for Richard to be done then we slowly walked home together. He didn't say anything about the little suitcase. He just walked with me. I guess no words were really necessary.

Coming through the back door, I dropped my suitcase in the laundry room and went into the kitchen. I opened the refrigerator and took out some vegetable that I thought would make an "interesting" salad. Lettuce, celery, green pepper, and some apples. It was the first time I had used apples in the salad. I made some sort of mayonnaise dressing and hoped for the best. Next, I set the table for a soup and salad type dinner.

Sitting around the dinner table everyone was contributing their own little chatter. I was quiet which was unusual. I sat next to my mother. She leaned over and quietly said, "So you decided not to run away?" I meekly said "Yes."

"Linda this is a very imaginative salad. You did a great job." At that moment I couldn't imagine that there was anywhere to run to that was better than where I was.

Running Away Redo

I had worked a long, hard day and was anxious to get home to my two children. I often felt guilty that they came home from school to an empty house. They were still pretty young to be staying alone, but I couldn't afford a baby-sitter and they were always where they were supposed to be when I got home. Brian was pretty much in charge, but they knew the rules and as far as I could tell, they kept within the boundaries of those rules.

As I came through town, I stopped at the Taco Bell. I didn't want to waste time cooking and they loved tacos, nachos and all those drive-thru treats. This would be good. We'd sit in front of the TV and watch a program of their choice. It was going to be a good night.

There was nothing different about my driveway or yard as I pulled up. The sun had gone down and there were lots of shadows on the grass from the big pine trees. Some of the trees had branches all the way down to the ground.

I went inside and set out the food on plates and then took them all out to the coffee table. I called for both kids and Brain came running out of his room. He bounced onto the coach and grabbed a taco. "Ohh, tacos!" he said as he grabbed the remote to find something to watch.

"Lisa!" I called. Nothing. "Brian, do you know where Lisa is?"

"She ran away today. Thanks for getting the nachos." He was matter of fact. Like she was just in the shower or taking a nap.

"WHAT! What do you mean she ran away? Where did she go?"

"I don't know. She packed some things and left." I couldn't believe his nonchalance.

I ran outside and called her name. No answer. I went to the backyard with my flashlight and searched there. She was not there. I walked the half-block up to the playground. No sign of her. Where could she have gone?

Frantic now, I ran inside and called my mother and sister-in-law to come help me search for her. They were on their way. Next I called 911. They also were on their way. I was surprised that my family arrived on the scene faster than the police. My family was 20 miles away and the police should have been much closer.

Mom and Carrot went out knocking on the neighbors doors, but returned with no news. The police were busy asking me all kinds of questions. I gave them a recent picture of her and explained that they always went to the playground after getting a snack after school. Then they would come home and wait for me while doing their homework. They were good kids and I'd never had that problem with them before.

Brian told the policeman that he and Lisa had an argument and when Lisa didn't get her way, she simply announced that she was running away. Brian thought she was kidding and would be back before it got dark. He knew she didn't like the dark. But, he was sure she'd be home any minute now.

Now it was the policeman's turn to search for her. While several went a block over and knocked on doors, one stayed behind and searched around the house.

Five minutes later, a policeman returned with a bundle in his arms. *LISA!* She was rubbing her eyes and looking around. I didn't know if I should hug her or slap her. I decided to wait until the morning to address the issue.

She had packed a laundry basket with some clothes and made herself a bed in the lower tree branches of the pine tree next to the fence. She fell asleep and didn't see my car pull into the driveway. She didn't mean to fall asleep, but she did.

I was happy that the next morning would be Saturday and I wouldn't be going to work.

We sat at the breakfast table and I explained that last night's incident could not happen again. They both knew what to do in case of an emergency. They could call me at work; they could call Aunt Carrot; they could call Grandma and someone would be able to help them. They can always go next door if they felt uncomfortable. I reprimanded Lisa for her choice of solutions when she clearly had other options.

She apologized and explained that she did not MEAN to stay away so long. She didn't know she was going to fall asleep.

Arguments happen between brothers and sisters. Arguments happen between all siblings. But, I scolded Brian for not telling me the minute I walked through the door. I scolded him for not being concerned when Lisa did not return by dark.

When we were done with the scolding and apologizing, I called Carrot and told her I was going to run away to the fabric store. At least I was letting someone know and I wouldn't be falling asleep in the middle of the polyester fill batting display.

THIS PAGE INTENTIONALLY LEFT BLANK.

MEET THE MADAME

This was my ultimate "runaway" experience. It came at the suggestion/insistence of an unlikely source. My father knew me very well. Better than I had ever imagined that he knew me and his urging me to run away was a huge surprise to me.

I had travelled across country with my two young children (for the third time) and had not yet found a house or a job. I had been looking for more than a month and I was so very tired. I was short tempered with the kids and feeling restless. To earn my keep at my parents' house, I cooked, cleaned, ran errands, etc. My mother was still working and she really appreciated the extra helping hand. My father had stopped going to work daily, but was still gone for much of the day.

The plan was that Mike, my husband, would come back from deployment to Groton, Connecticut, and his orders would be waiting for him to be transferred to somewhere on the West Coast. I was to move back to the Bay Area and set up housekeeping. Even if he was stationed at San Diego, he would still be home at least one or two weekends a month, as well as his leave/vacation time. It wasn't ideal, but we would both be closer to our families and that was our prime objective.

Daddy and I always had breakfast together every morning. Sometimes he would cook and sometimes I would cook. It didn't matter, I loved our breakfasts together. Once particular morning, Daddy said to me that I looked like hell. Oh! Flattery will get you everywhere! He said it looked like I could use a change of scenery. I responded with reminding him that now would not be the time to be changing scenery. I was in the middle of job hunting, house hunting, etc. and I had the kids to think about. Besides, where would I go?

Daddy was part owner of a bar/restaurant in Tonopah, NV. I thought it was the Tonopah Saloon, but now I believe it was The Clubhouse. It still exists and has a lot of history. Tonopah is famous for being exactly half-way between Las Vegas and Reno, as well as, silver mines and bordellos. I think this saloon was once owned by Wyatt Earp, but I'm not sure about that.

It always seemed odd to me that my father would be involved in this type of establishment since he was neither a drinker nor a gambler. I believe it was a barter situation where someone had hired my Dad to do some soil investigation work but couldn't afford to pay the tab. So he handed over a part of the saloon in payment. Whatever. It didn't last all that long because Dad sold his share within a few years.

My father said "Jim Butler Days are coming up in Tonopah. You could go and work in the club, earn some extra money, and get away for a week or so. Mom and I will take care of the kids." At first, I resisted. No. Can't do that. Need to focus here. Blah. Blah. Blah. In the end I packed my bags and left for Nevada.

My father made all the arrangements. I arrived late, checked into my room and fell promptly asleep. When I opened my eyes, I was staring directly at the clock. 11 AM!! I never slept that late! I'm an early riser and was shocked to see that I had slept so late. I quickly dressed and headed out to explore the Tonopah. Well… there is really only the one street in Tonopah – Main Street.

My exploration ended at the Clubhouse. I went in and found the manager, introduced myself and she directed me to the bar where I introduced myself to the bartenders and wait staff. It was friendly place, the people all greeted me and said "Oh! You're Morris' daughter!" Then the conversations would start as though they had known me my whole life.

There was an attractive woman sitting on the barstool next to me. She was playing with the straw of her drink – which turned out to be a simple iced tea – no liquor added. She turned to me and said, "Welcome to Tonopah, Linda. How long are you going to be in town?" I told her it would just be a week or two, then I had to get back to my kids. "I would love for you to come out to the ranch for lunch. But, it's Jim Butler Days and we'll be really busy." Oh. That's very nice of her to ask, but I understand that ranch life is very busy this time of year.

"I'm Beverly Harrell, owner of the Cottontail Ranch. We don't have cows or horses, just lovely ladies who are paid for their services. We're moving off the BLM land and down the road to a different property. So things are really hectic. Besides that, I'm running for Nevada Assemblywoman."

Now, I knew that prostitution was legal in Nevada, but never had I thought that I would be sipping ice tea with one of the madams of a local institution. We talked until it was well into the dinner hour and a group of us gathered at a table and was served what seemed to be a never-ending supply of delicious plates on the menu. No one ordered. The food just kept on coming.

The bar was starting to fill up with patrons. Bells on slot machines rang more frequently now. Voices and music were louder now. The diners disappeared from the table and Beverly and I were alone. She told me about my father telling her that I would be a good addition to Beverly's campaign team. But, he made sure she understood that I would never be interested in working as one of her "girls." We decided to see how I liked Tonopah and if I would be interested in relocating there.

The evening ended and I left for the peace and quiet of my room. The next day, I would be working in the bar and knew I had to get some rest to be up for the task.

It had been years since I had done any waitressing and I was a little uncertain if my experience would match what was needed. Instead of waiting tables, I was assigned to waiting the slots. It was pretty simple. Drinks at the slots were free, so I didn't have to deal with that. However, I provided change for people when they wanted to convert bills into coins. It was simple and the tips were fantastic. I wore a little red frilly uniform which revealed more that I wanted of my cleavage and legs. But, it was fun. The customers were fun and as long as I kept them happy, it was an easy job.

Over the next week, I expanded my duties to waiting dinner tables and bar tables. On the weekend there was a band and the crowd was a lot rowdier. But the lead server always watched over me and ran interference when some of the men got to hands-on or loud-mouthed. At the shift's end, we would gather at a dining table, be fed sinfully large amounts of scrumptious food, drink coffee and talk.

Ms. Harrell learned of my impending departure and came to the saloon for my last night. I thanked her for the job offer, but I felt I needed to be closer to my family in California. I didn't want to uproot my kids again and take them away from their grandparents. I wished her luck in her pursuit of Assemblywoman and told her I believed she would be the candidate I would vote for if I were a resident of Nevada.

I arrived home with some jingle in my pocket – actually it didn't jingle because it was bills and not just coin. Financially, it was time well spent. I felt renewed in that, although I was tired, I was ready to continue my search for a job with fresh confidence. After all, not everyone gets offered a job as a Madam's assistance in her race for the assembly.

Over breakfast, I asked my father if he had set me up to meet Beverly and be offered the job. He said he may have had a hand in it a bit. He knew if he had told me about Beverly that I might not understand and be offended. So he took a less obvious route. He didn't think I would take the job, but wanted me to have an opportunity that was outside the box of my norm.

My parents were going to Tonopah the next weekend. Before they left, I asked my Mom if she knew Beverly and knew of her "ranch". My mother told me that, of course, she knew Beverly and that she had been out to the ranch. She was happy I had met her. She added that it brought home that anyone could be anything in this country. Who would have thought that a madam could run for a political position?

Beverly won the race, but something happened in the overnight ballot counting and the next day, she was declared to NOT have won. The whole incident caused there to be a questionable light on the race. But, Beverly did not take office. However, she is probably most publicized madam in the history books.

Thank you Daddy for sending me to Tonopah. Thank you Beverly, "Nevada's Fighting Madam", for expanding my knowledge base and offering me an outstanding, yet unusual and unorthodox, opportunity.

Madame Beverly Baird Harrell
B 6/2/1929 – D 9/4/1995

THIS PAGE INTENTIONALLY LEFT BLANK.

This space is left so that you can write your own interesting characters in your life.

SCHEDULE? WE HAVE A SCHEDULE?

I loved taking trips and travelling with my mother. She was an adventurer. When the opportunity presented itself to us to drive across country, I jumped at it. I was moving from Portsmouth, VA back to California with my son, age 6, my daughter age 3 and my Polydactyl cat named Pauzz. I bought a plane ticket for Mom to fly out and so she could help me prepare for the trip.

We poured over my atlas and discussed routes. It was August and we choose the southern route because I had to make a stop in Atlanta to pick up some papers and back child support from my ex-husband. Our trip had us going straight to Atlanta and travel along the coast of Florida, Alabama, Mississippi. Then we would head to Morgan City, Louisiana, where we my father was working. Then we'd travel into Texas where we would visit with Great Aunt Alma. Then we would go across New Mexico, Arizona and northerly into California. It was a good route. It was a good plan and we were so excited about this trip.

The movers came and packed up the house. We followed the big moving van out of our quaint little neighborhood and out to the interstate. We were on our way!

In Atlanta, I found a lumber mill where I purchased a piece of plywood. The millers cut to the shape and size of my back seat of my 1969 Toronado. It covered three-quarters of the seat and the rest of the area was open. A person could still sit up in the back, but after laying down a piece of soft foam and a quilt, it was a perfect area for the kids to nap or play. Under the board were the cat's box, food and water. The cat could hide away if it didn't like the activity in the back seat.

183

We left early in the morning. It was the way my mother and I always started road trips. We leave as early as possible and drive for several hours before stopping for breakfast. Then we'd get back in the car and drive until our tummy was hitting our backbones and stop to eat again. We figured with both of us driving alternately, this trip would be over before we knew it. But we didn't take into account how much fun we were about to have.

I was resting in the passenger seat. The kids were napping in the back. The cat was nowhere to be seen. I heard the crunch driving on gravel and opened my eyes to see us pulling into what looked like a Mom & Pop variety store. "We need some snacks and sodas." Mom said. I told her I would wait here with the kids. Then off she went, into the store. It seemed like she had been in there for hours before she reappeared with several bags. She motioned me to come look. I went to the trunk and she was pulling clothes out of the bag. There were little dresses and outfits for both Brian and Lisa. Then she showed me the price tag and I was shocked at how inexpensive the treasures were. WOW! What a find! We would definitely keep our eyes open for more little variety stores.

Three or four stores later, we pulled into our first motel of the trip. We were in Mobile, Alabama, at a small motel right on the Gulf Coast. It was a courtyard of small white cottages, each with a front porch and rocking chair. There were orchids everywhere in the landscaping and Magnolia Trees strategically placed between each cottage. There was a carport between each cottage. I felt that we may have inadvertently been transported back to the 1950's. In the morning, there was a tray of fresh coffee and cinnamon rolls, a newspaper and fresh orchids mixed with other flowers. Oh, we wanted to stay another night just to see what would be on our porch the next morning. But, we had to move on. The owner of the motel, a sweet man with a straw fedora, told us not to miss Bellingrath Gardens. We checked our map and decided it would be our next stop.

It was the most beautiful place I had ever seen. Just like something from "Gone with the Wind." There was moss hanging from the trees that lined the mile long driveway. We pulled into the parking lot and pulled out the stroller and the cat. Pauzz was placed in the facility kennel with his food and water. Lisa was put into the stroller after a lot of resistance. We purchased our tickets and was handed a map of the garden paths, ponds, trails along with descriptions of what to watch for during our tour.

Brian insisted upon pushing the stroller and Lisa was quietly enjoying the ride. We came upon a pond with stepping stones across and around through water lily pads with beautiful flowers. It appeared to be a maze of large plants with the stones leading the way. We certainly couldn't take the stroller and debated about whether or not Lisa had a stride long enough to reach each stone. She was too heavy to be carried. We took her out of the stroller and told her to only step to the next stone when Mommy told her to. OK. She agreed. It was so breath-taking to be out in this pond with plants all around us. I would lift Lisa and hand her over to Mom at each step. Brian was in the lead. It was like playing a game of leap frog across the pond.

I don't know if I mentioned that Lisa has a mind of her own. Even at age three she knew exactly what she wanted and was insistent at getting what she wanted. I turned back to reach for her but she had already tried taking that step – and was now sinking in the water. All I could see was her little pony tail rising to the top of the water. I reached down and pulled her out using her hair like a rope. I didn't think that I could be pulling the kid's hair out of her head. I really didn't think at all – I just acted. I acted quickly and without reservation. She was screaming. I grabbed her up and ran across the stones over to her stroller. I used her blanket to dry her off. Our time at Bellingrath Gardens had come to an abrupt end.

Mom re-dressed Lisa and cuddled her close. Brian and I went to retrieve Mr. Pauzz but he was NOT in the kennel. Brian started calling for him and big tears were streaming down his face. We had lost our beloved Pauzz. We gathered up his food and water bowls and went back to the car. Brian kept calling for him… "PAUZZ!! PAUZZ!! Come on boy! Come on back!" But, Pauzz didn't appear. That is – he didn't appear until we got back to the car where he crawled out from under our car and rubbed himself between Brian's legs.

Lisa was dry and Pauzz was back. All was right with the world. Time to move on down the road.

As we travelled to Interstate 10, we made several more "little variety store" stops. I couldn't resist all the cute little outfits at such a small cost. At this rate, I'd have Brian all ready for school before we ever got back to California. Of course, all the stops were slowing us down a bit, but I didn't feel that we were on a time clock. Well, my father didn't feel the same way.

When we arrived in Morgan City my father had a scowl on his face. We were so excited to see him, but he admonished us for being so tardy. We were more than a day late and he had been very worried. He reminded us that we needed to get back to California because school would be starting soon. I needed to get the kids registered and ready to go.

I think part of his being upset was the fact that we were two women travelling alone with two small children. These were the days before cell phones and emergency call boxes. Although, he knew we were competent to handle the trip, he was worried about something happening and us being left vulnerable. We told him we would do as he asked and be more vigilant about reaching our destination.

We left Morgan City and headed northwest towards Bangs, Texas where we would visit with my paternal grandmother's sister, Great Aunt Alma. We were very mindful of my father's worries about safety and made sure we stopped for the night half-way between the two towns. It really wasn't a very long drive, less than 10 hours, but we wanted to be fresh for our visit.

Looking at Aunt Alma was like looking at my Grandmother Nora. It wasn't that they really looked all that much alike. It was just knowing that this woman was the sister of someone who had been so very important in my life. Her husband was tall and sturdy and had a great sense of humor. They lived on a family farm and I imagined my father's family living on a farm much like Aunt Alma's. It was very flat and dry. I could see for miles beyond the barn and farming equipment. It was a wonderful visit, but time for us to get back on the road.

Continuing to drive northwest towards Lubbock, Mom and I started thinking about all the cattle that was raised in Texas. That lead us to thinking about steak. We had been eating so much seafood, sandwiches, hamburgers and barbeque, but had not had any real beef since we left Portsmouth. It seemed logical to us that we should be able to find incredible steaks in Texas. We were now on a mission to find a restaurant with awesome steaks. We stopped for gas and asked several people, each with their own opinion about the best steakhouse around. We settled on one that was on our route.

We settled ourselves in the booth and looked over the menu. We knew what Lisa would be ordering. Brian always waited until he found out what Mom and I were ordering. Mom and I looked at each other. There was no REAL steak on the menu. BBQ, burgers, pork chops, BBQ ribs – but no rib eyes, porterhouse, T-bone, New York Strip. We promptly left the booth and headed for another steakhouse. On our way out, we asked a patron if they knew of any other places to get a really good steak. They gave us directions and we went hunting for our slab of beef.

After about an hour drive, we found the establishment that proudly proclaimed to having juicy steaks as written across the windows. Once again, we settled into a booth, read the menu and told the waitress we were ready to order.

Of course, Mom and I ordered steak and Brian ordered a steak as well. When Lisa was asked what she wanted for dinner, she promptly said "I'll have a cheeseburger with no cheese and French fries." The waitress replied with "Oh, you want a hamburger? Right?" Lisa indignantly said NO! She wanted a cheeseburger with no cheese." I let the waitress know she was on the right track and she went off to get our food.

From the very start of the trip, Lisa always ordered the exact same thing. It didn't matter if it was breakfast, lunch or dinner – she wanted a cheeseburger with no cheese. Somehow she got into her mind that it was not the same thing as a hamburger. We indulged in her little idiosyncrasy and she ate cheeseburgers with no cheese all the way across the country.

The salads were fresh and the blue cheese dressing was certainly homemade. Lisa was loving her cheeseburger (WITHOUT cheese). Our steaks arrived and they smelled delicious. They smelled good. They looked good. Our mouths were watering. They were as tough as the leather on the sole of your shoe. WHAT?? I had a rib steak and Mom had a T-bone. How in the world could they be so tough? We chewed up as best we could because we were starving and to wait for another steak, which could be just as bad as the first, would have meant starving for a little while longer. We complained when we paid our bill, and was given a discount. As we were leaving, we stopped a man with a dog in his truck. He had finished his meal as well and he looked happy – he must not have ordered steak. We asked if his dog would like our doggie boxes and he graciously accepted.

Very close to the restaurant was a motel and we decided to check in for the night. The next morning we had breakfast at a little diner. We both ordered their special – steak and eggs. The steak was melt-in-your mouth wonderful and full of flavor. Our craving had finally been satisfied.

We were on our way now! Still travelling northwest up to Interstate 40, we planned on not making any other sightseeing or shopping stops until got to California. Our little search for steak had put us more than a day behind and my father's words were still ringing in my ears.

I don't remember exactly what was wrong with the car, but there was some kind break down. We were still, very near the border of New Mexico. We were stopped alongside the road and I knew I needed water for the radiator. Two off-duty Texas Rangers stopped and offered us some help. They were life savers. They called for a tow truck, but all of us into their big double cab truck and off we went. The closest town was Clovis, NM. The car was dropped off at a garage and we were taken to the closest motel.

Back in 1974 Clovis didn't really have much going on for itself. There was a museum and a movie theater, but other than that, the town was pretty dead. Fortunately, there was a pool at the motel. Without the pool, I think we would have died of boredom. The mechanic had good news and bad news. He could fix he car, but he had to order the part and it would take THREE days to get it. We had no choice but to wait for the part.

There was a mini-frig and a hot plate in the room. When the hotel management found out our situation, they offered us a discount on the room cost. Mom took a taxi to the grocery store so we could eat without spending money on taxi fare for every meal. Anyone who has experience my mother's kitchen ability knows she can cook anything anywhere with very little and it will taste like a five-star meal. The next three days were spent watching cartoons, playing cards and swimming. Actually, it was a welcome break after all the driving.

As promised, the car was fixed and delivered to our motel on the fourth day. We were ready to get the hell out of Dodge – or Clovis as was our case.

That was it. No more dilly-dallying. We would take turns driving straight through as much as possible. We would make no more than two overnight stops between Clovis and Brentwood, California. We were full-steam ahead.

Kids get restless. They are not designed to be quiet and patient no matter how tricked out the back seat of a Toronado may be. They started arguing and I could hear both myself and Mom telling them over and over to stop, quiet down, settle down, don't hit your sister (or brother), and on, and on, and on. Their little kid ears could not hear us. We were in the Painted Desert and we tried to get them to look at all the beautiful colors on the mountains. But they weren't interested. "If you two don't stop fussing and fighting, I'm going to pull over and put you out. You can walk all the way to California!" I had reached the end of my rope. They did not stop. "Do you want me to stop this car?" They still did not stop. I warned them again and when they did not stop, I pulled the car off to the side of the road.

Quiet. Everything suddenly got very quiet. Then tears started as I opened their car door. Whaaat? Mommy what are you doing? Why are we getting out? NO! Please Mommy. Grandma please help us. I reminded them of all the times I told them I would put them out if they did not behave. Oh… you were serious about that? Please don't leave us… I can still hear their little pleas as I got back into the driver's seat. I was watching their little faces and trying not to let them see that I was crying harder than they were. My mother watched… she watched me and she watched them. She adjusted her side mirror so she could clearly see them.

Slowly, I drove off at about 10 mph. I could see them in the rear view mirror. Their little legs were running now, trying to catch up to the car. I drove just to the top of the next rise and watched them. There was no traffic and I had been mindful of that before letting them out. It was very early in the morning so it was still cool. They had been out of the car for less than five minutes by the time they caught up to us. I got out of the car and went around to the passenger door. "When Mommy or Grandma says to quiet down and stop fighting, are you going to do as we ask?" Both nodded and said "Yes, Mommy." I then asked if they thought they could behave for the rest of the trip?" Both responded with a promise to be good.

That few minutes in the middle of the Painted Desert was probably enough trauma to give fodder to a psychiatrist for the rest of their lives. I'm sure, if they had abandonment issues, they probably were created that day. However, it also generated enough guilt in me to convince me that I was the most horrible, terrible mother that ever existed. For months afterward, I was very careful to let them know exactly where I was going and when I would return and I left them as seldom as possible. When I did leave them, it was only with a family member that they trusted.

The rest of the trip was uneventful. We didn't make any sightseeing stops or shopping side trips. After the car repair, we didn't have the funds to play. We arrived in Brentwood, CA, after almost three weeks of travel. The straight trip would only have taken us about five days. But, we tripled the time.

We had tons of photos to develop at one of those drive-through photo booths. It costs more than $100 to develop them all. We certainly didn't need that many photos, but, oh well… we had them.

The bags were not completely unpacked from the car for several days. We just took in our primary suitcases. I wanted to give Pauzz a chance to get acclimated to the new residence before we had too much activity around the car. We left the window down for him so he could come and go. We didn't anticipate a relative arriving with a super-king sized dog. At that particular time, Pauzz was standing on the ground outside the car window. The dog saw the cat and the chase was on in full force. Pauzz didn't make it back into the car. He was gone. We searched for days and never found him. Brian would go out looking for him, but always returned without him. I told him we could get another cat, but that didn't console him. It took a long time for him to recover from the loss.

I've travelled across country many times in my lifetime. No trip has ever compared to the one I took with my mother. It was a bonding experience for a mother and daughter who were very close to begin with. I wish we could do it again. I wish she were here to read this story. Thank you, Mom, for being my co-pilot.

I CAN FIX THIS

Ben lived just a few houses up the street from us. He was the same age as my brother, Richard. After school they would ride their bikes up and down our street, down the dirt road and into the orchards. They would come back all dusty and dirty, but satisfied for getting out all those classroom frustrations with a hard and fast bike ride.

The two boys told my mother they were going for a ride and would be back later. As usual my mother yelled at them to be careful and stay away from the canal. Her biggest fear was that one of them would fall into the fast moving water and swept away. All of us kids were warned of the canal from the minute we could understand English. We were all sufficiently afraid to venture too close to the concrete river.

Richard and Ben had been gone for quite some time when Ben appeared back at our house. "Mrs. Bartee? Could I have a Band-Aid? Richard fell off his bike and scrapped his knee." My mother got him several Band-Aids and turned them over to Ben. He promptly got back on his bike and rode off towards the dirt road.

Mom waited patiently for the boys to return. She was anxious to see the damage to Richard's knee. When the boys didn't return, she decided it must have been just a simple little scrape. Just as she was convincing herself that everything was OK, Ben re-appeared in the kitchen. "I think I need a few more bandages." Ben explained. My mother asked him if he was sure they didn't need her help. "Oh no," he insisted.

This time when Ben left, Mom noted the time in her head. If they could truly handle the situation, then she wanted to not interfere in finding a solution to their problem. She told herself it was all in the process of allowing kids to grow up. But, when an hour had gone by, she gave up on all that and got in the car. She drove about half-way down the dirt road when she came upon Ben and Richard. Richard's bike was a tangled mess and Richard was lying back in the dirt with tears streaming down his face leaving mud trails down his cheeks.

"What happened here?" Mom said. "Looks like you're gonna need more than a couple of bandages." She kneeled down and inspected Richard's knee. Pieces of cartilage hung from the wound and the area around the knee-cap looked like hamburger. Dirt and stones were imbedded in what was left of his knee. Ben helped her get Richard into the car and then loaded his bike in the trunk. Mom drove off towards home, but knew she'd be going to Dr. Kaplan's office.

With Richard at home, Mom could really clean out the injury and remove the stones, twigs and dirt. She bandaged it by wrapping it in gauze. She couldn't get the bleeding to stop. It was time to call the doctor. It was close to 6 p.m. so she knew she would have to call the answering service. Dr. Kaplan returned her call almost immediately and told her to meet him at the office.

To the rest of us kids, it seemed a very long time before Mom and Richard returned. Richard's knee was cleaned and packed with gauze and wrapped in an ace bandage. He had crutches and was instructed to stay off his feet. All of us kids knew that meant he wouldn't be doing any dinner dishes and they we would be assigned to wait on him hand and foot – literally. However, our sarcasm waned when Mom changed the bandage and we could see how much of his knee just wasn't there anymore.

Over a period of time, he had surgery to cut away the dead tissue and there was speculation that he would not be able to walk properly again.

Ben visited almost daily. The two played checkers and other board games. They watched TV and talked about things that all teen boys talk about. Eventually he got better and was able to walk without crutches. For the rest of his life he favored that knee and walked with a bit of a limp. But at least he could walk.

I don't think Ben realized when he asked for that Band-Aid, that he was going to need a lot more than that to fix Richard's little scrape. The important thing to remember is that Ben did not abandon him. He stayed with his friend and helped him get to a place where he was able to ride his bike again. Although, I don't remember them hauling out of the drive-way at the speed of light again.

THIS PAGE INTENTIONALLY LEFT BLANK.

I Didn't Do It

Brian was my quiet, easy child. Pregnancy and delivery were easy. Potty-training and bottle-breaking were easy transitions. Even his first day of school was simple for him while I had tears streaming down my face. He was beautiful with his long blonde curls framing his sweet face. His smile could light up the room. That's not to say that he didn't have a side to him that was… well… a bit devious. He was the master of unexpected surprises creating a bit of drama when all things appeared to be calm.

There was the time when both kids chores included making sure the kitchen was clean before I got home from work. It was the one thing that I insisted upon. I refused to cook in a dirty kitchen and I didn't run out for fast food just because the dishes were not done. They were to take turns. There was never a LOT of dishes and we had a dishwasher.

The schedule was simple. First homework, then kitchen, then play until the streetlights came on, come home, eat dinner, take a bath and go to bed. One day Brian decided he didn't like the schedule and was in a hurry. He quickly stacked all the dishes under the sink and ran out the door. When I returned home, it appeared that the kitchen chore had been done. I cooked dinner and everything seemed fine.

The next day, when I came home from work, it looked as though Lisa had done her dish duty correctly. However – when I opened the cabinet under the sink, I saw stacks of dirty dishes. It wasn't a lot, but there they were, all stacked up and out of sight. My first thought was that Lisa had done it. Those were her dishes under the sink. It didn't occur to me that they had been there more than one day.

As punishment Lisa was to do all the dinner dishes along with the ones under the sink. She was forced to not watch TV and wait for the dishwasher to finish and then put away the clean ones. Lisa protested, she stomped her feet, she cried alligator tears, all the time insisting that it was Brian who shirked his responsibility. Lisa was always over the top dramatic. I figured she was just making excuses.

Brian was minding his own business when the discovery was made. He said nothing. He glanced up every once and a while, but did not come to his sister's defense. Lisa was yelling at him "Brian! Brian! Tell Mom the truth, Brian! Come on, Brian!" I ignored it, but out of the corner of my eye I caught him smile as she was pleading with him. AHHH!!! HAAA!!! I knew in an instant that Brian was my culprit.

Lisa had already started on her punishment and I stopped her abruptly. Brian was told he would have the punishment assigned to his sister, but he would also not watch TV for three days. Since he was trying to get Lisa to take the blame, he had to do her chores for the rest of the week. Lisa was vindicated and let Brian know with little sarcastic jabs. "I think I'll use a clean plate for my chips" or "looks like you forgot this one."

Brian, my sweet angel, had a devilish side to him, but he always got caught. He was not good at deception.

One time I had taken Lisa and Brian to spend a week in a cabin on the lake. There was a pier that had a ladder to a dock. The kids would jump into the water from there and toast their white bodies in the sun. The water wasn't very deep. It wasn't deep enough for diving, but fine for jumping.

I was taking some pictures and asked the two of them to stand together at the edge of the dock. I took several pictures while Brian asked a dozen questions. This was unusual because Lisa was the noisy one. I turned my back for just a second and I heard a splash accompanied with screams. I turned back and Brian was alone on the dock still standing in the position he had when I had turned away. Lisa was standing in the lake. She was on her tip toes trying to keep her head above water. I went over and helped fish her out and bank onto the deck.

"Brian! How could you do that! I could have drowned! Mom, do something!" Lisa was livid with her brother. While she was ranting, Brian was calmly saying he thought she would think it was fun. He was just playing with her. I guess I should have been angry, but instead I saw it as an opportunity. Lisa was screaming, Brian was laughing and I reached up and pushed Brian off the dock. The shock of my actions set both of them off. They were laughing and yelling at me that I was not being fair. I ran off knowing if they caught me, I'd be in the water next.

Brian & Lisa 1973

THIS PAGE INTENTIONALLY LEFT BLANK.

Kids will be kids.

JUST A LITTLE SNACK

My son, Brian, was a funny person. I don't mean he was funny as in weird. He was funny as in comedic. What made him even funnier was that he didn't realize he was funny. He didn't have to try, he just was.

Lisa and her family had moved to North Carolina from California. Once they were settled, she invited Brian to come and stay a while. He was more than happy to come for a visit.

By the time he got there, his nephew had met the girlfriend of his dreams and the two high-schoolers were just starting what would be a very, very long term relationship. However, the kids were not allowed to be inside the house alone when there was not an adult present.

Brian was sitting on the front porch with the kids and asked why they didn't go inside. "We're not allowed when there is no adult." Brian, a bit put out because he was four years older than his sister, responded with "What am I, chopped liver? Go inside if you want. In fact, do you want a snack. I'll fix you a snack."

They all went inside, put a movie on and Brian went to the kitchen to prepare a snack. Hmmm…. What to fix? Then he found the perfect snack food. It took a while to prepare, but the smell from the kitchen made the kids mouth water.

Brian's idea of a snack was to cook a whole spiral ham complete with glaze. When his nephew saw what Brian had prepared he was surprised. After all, they were expecting, maybe, a peanut butter and jelly sandwich. "I think you better call Mom and tell her you cooked her ham."

Lisa answered the phone and heard, "Uhhh, Lisa? What were you going to cook for dinner tonight? Because, if it was ham, I just did you a huge favor. All you have to cook is the sides. I've done everything else."

"I'm so lucky to have you as a brother! Thank you." Lisa replied.

Brian turned to the kids and said, "How's that for dodging a bullet? Unless you tell them that I wasn't even thinking about dinner, they will never know. You're not going to tell her are you?"

"Well... I don't like to lie to Mom. You know she always finds out. But... what's our snack going to be tomorrow?" his nephew asked with a raised eyebrow and crocked smile.

Brian – Wanna snack? Let me fix you a little snack.

RECIPES

When my brother married Carolyn (long before she became Carrot) she had not had much experience with meal preparation. She could do a few things like scrambled eggs, salami sandwiches, hamburgers and hot dogs. But w4hen she was growing up the family of three seldom sat down and actually had a home-cooked meal prepared by her mother. It wasn't that her mom (Hannah) wasn't a good cook – quite the opposite – her mother was an outstanding cook. Hannah's prime rib roast was the best I have ever tasted to this very day. Her recipe was a secret that she did not share even as she was on her death bed.

The problem was that Hannah worked all the time, day and night, to provide for her two children. There was little time for super table chat, let alone fancy meals. The two kids learned to adapt. They learned to cook the things that kids like to eat or they simply got something from the restaurant where Hannah was working.

Now that Carolyn was a married woman with a husband who had a regular full meal at super time each and every night, she was going to have to learn a few tricks. Newly wedded bliss was wonderful but it didn't fill that place where food was supposed to be. Carolyn was smart. She knew what she had to do. She asked her mother-in-law to help her learn to cook a few dishes that were Richard's favorite.

A little bit of background here: My father insisted that the family eat liver at least twice a month. He also insisted upon a salad every single night. We fellow diners were ecstatic about the salad because it would cover up the taste of the liver. As a child, liver, to me, was simply fried shoe leather. My older brother, Richard, on the other hand, loved liver night. He couldn't get enough of it. So he didn't care if there was salad because he was happy just to eat the meat.

My mother was an excellent cook. Out of all the things that she excelled at, cooking was the one that always got everyone's attention. The saying goes that she could turn a simple dinner for four into a banquet for twelve. Unlike, Hannah, my mother was always willing to share all her recipes with anyone who expressed an interest. If you asked her for a recipe, she would beam with pride that someone thought so much of her cooking. She didn't learn to cook until she married my father and she did just about the same thing that Carolyn was about to do.

Carolyn asked my mother what she could fix for Richard that would really impress him. My mother had just gone grocery shopping and offered to give Carolyn some liver for dinner that evening. Carolyn hesitated. Really? Liver? Lois wanted her to cook LIVER? But Carolyn was a willing student. OK. Let's cook up a batch of liver.

Lois explained that Carolyn must always use calves liver and not regular liver. She told her to soak the liver in buttermilk. While the liver was taking a buttermilk bath, Lois cut up almost a whole bag of yellow onions. Then she fried a whole pound of bacon and when it was done, she dumped the cut onions into the bacon grease. The heat was turned down and the onions were allowed to just quietly become soft and brown.

The house smelled of bacon and onions and the aroma made Carolyn hungry. How bad could the live be if it starts out like this? Carolyn peeled a bag of potatoes and put them in a pot of salted water. This would be mashed potatoes.

With the onions and bacon fried and the potatoes almost boiling, Lois turned her attention to the salad. She told Carolyn that a good salad can make even a mediocre meal feel complete. Carrot chopped up tomatoes, green peppers, green onions and shredded some carrots. The salad looked beautiful as she added just a touch of oil and vinegar.

Lois showed Carolyn the best way she knew to mash up the potatoes. After draining off the water, leave them in the hot pan and add a stick of butter (real butter – not margarine). Salt, pepper and just a touch of nutmeg. Next use the potato masher and squish the potatoes into a white mush. Now add some milk to make them creamier. Put the lid on the pan and set the pan back in a warm place on the stove.

Carolyn was told to watch carefully because liver was a delicate meat to cook. A paper bag was opened up and filled with flour, salt and pepper along with just a tiny bit of corn meal. Each piece of meat was put into the bag and coated with a quick shaking of the closed bag. The process continued until each piece was coated.

Lois used the same pan as the bacon and onions and added a bit more bacon grease. After the grease was very hot, Lois gently placed each piece into the pan. Carolyn could hear the liver sizzle as it joined the hot cast iron skillet. It seemed only a matter of seconds when Lois turned the meat over and fried the other side. Each piece of meat took only about five minutes to cook.

Lois made a gravy was made from the pan drippings. With all the food ready for serving, Lois explained how the food would most likely be eaten. She placed a heaping helping of potatoes on the plate. The liver was placed on top of the potatoes and was smothered by the bacon and onions. Next the gravy was drizzled over the top. Add a vegetable – any vegetable would do. Put the salad in a separate bowl. If she wanted to really impress Richard give him strawberries and whipped cream for dessert.

The dinner looked delicious even though it was liver. Carolyn tasted a few bites and found that it was surprisingly really good. She rushed home to make her new husband one of his favorite meals.

Richard LOVED his dinner that night. He said he liked it so much, that he would love to have it again soon.

"Mom? I was wondering if you could do me a favor." Richard asked. "I was wondering if you could teach Carolyn how to make a few more dishes. Like your goulash. Goulash would be great. We've had liver three times a week now for the past four weeks."

Lois laughed until her sides split. She then got out her notebook and began making a cookbook of all of Richard's favorite foods.

GET IT RIGHT

Lisa makes a wonderful hamburger rolled up in pastry dough type dish. When she first tried making it, it wasn't so good. She had no recipe. A friend of hers had a gathering and served it as an appetizer. Lisa fell in love with it and decided she needed to learn to make it. But she did not want to ask for the recipe. She decided she could figure it out on her own.

Because she didn't have much of a kitchen at her place, she would drop over after work and experiment with making the hamburger roll. Then she would serve it for us as the dinner meal.

At first she was making the burger roll every day for about a week. Then she dropped down to every couple of days. She would try to change it up a bit each time, hoping to come up with the perfect burger roll recipe. And we were all her guinea pigs.

My nephew heard me on the phone with Lisa but wasn't sure what we were talking about. After we hung up, he requested an opportunity to talk to me.

"Aunt Linda, could you please tell Lisa not to cook dinner for us tonight? Or could you please tell her not to cook that hamburger thing again? We would really love to have some of YOUR clam chowder or fried chicken. Please."

I told him I would cook for them anything they wanted that night – it was both clam chowder and fried chicken. But, I also told him that I would let Lisa make one more burger roll. When she served it, everyone was to tell her it was the best one she has made yet and that she should not do any more improvements to the recipe.

She was so elated that she had accomplished her goal that she didn't make another hamburger roll for several years.

SECURITY RISK

Because my husband was on a fast-attack submarine, he held a top secret security clearance. I really didn't think it had anything to do with me. It was his deal, his job, his status. I couldn't have been more wrong.

Mike was deployed overseas. For a submariner that means the sailor is out of contact. Literally. This was before cell phones, e-mail, tweeting, or Skype. Communication was maintained between spouses via the good old snail mail system. When the boat was out to sea, not moored at any port, there was no mail in or out. Letters from the wives were still mailed and a date was put on the outside of the envelope so the sailor knew in which order to open them. Men would receive mail in batches. The spouses would usually just get a letter a day for about ten days, and then... nothing for weeks on end. During those long dry spells, the same letters were read over and over again. Our letters ran the gauntlet of newsy, sweet and loving to downright x-rated. Sometimes we would even argue through the mail system. It was OK. Everyone was just happy to have something in the mail box.

I was working a part-time job. I came home from work one day to find two well-dressed men sitting in my living room with the baby-sitter. I was happy I had just come from work because I was dressed professionally. If I had just been spending the day at home, I would have been in baggy jeans and a T-shirt. Being in a dress and heels made me feel like I was more on equal ground. They stood up as I entered the room. I stated that I was Linda and extended my hand as I asked if I could help them with something. They introduced themselves. I don't remember their names now, so I'll just call them Moe and Joe.

They told me they were following up on Mike's security status and needed to interview me as a part of the process. OK. I thought that made sense and I really had nothing to hide.

I was asked if I had ever been on-board the submarine. Of course, I had many times. I went there whenever Mike had to serve a 24 hour duty set. I would go for dinner and we would visit until sunset and then I would go home. I found the inside of the sub to be very confining and didn't like to stay for long. Whenever I was there, I focused on Mike and not the surroundings.

When Moe and Joe asked what I had SEEN during my visits to the sub, I couldn't really give them specifics. To me, the whole inside looked like it was packed with grey and black boxes. There was a glass type table where the periscope was, but other than that; I wasn't sure what to tell them. So I told them the truth.

When I said black boxes – I thought Moe and Joe's eyes would pop out of their heads. They started asking me question after question about those boxes. Did Mike ever talk about them? Did he tell me what they were used for? What did I know about those boxes?

Come on... they were just boxes of all different sizes and shapes. Mike and I never discussed them except he did tell me they contained electronic stuff. I didn't really care what was in them. I have to admit I did enjoy looking through the periscope. The huge light table used for navigational mapping was something I could envision using in drafting sewing patterns. But what interested me most when I visited Mike onboard was what was on the galley's dinner menu. On Friday night's they served lobster and that was my favorite night to visit.

The men ended the interview and I thought the whole thing was over. WRONG! They were waiting on my doorstep a few days later after I had done some grocery shopping. They helped me bring in my bags and watched as I put away the food. In celebration of a co-worker's birthday, I was planning a special dinner. I had gotten some fresh crab legs for the occasion. They took special interest in those crabs. How could I afford crab on a petty officer's salary? I reminded them that I also brought money into the house. Who was the co-worker? What was our relationship? Could they see my bank statements? Why wasn't Mike and I married yet?

I was clearly getting irritated and told them if they wanted more information they would have to bring something tangible that gave them the right to inspect my personal life. I took the sleeve of each one and guided them to the door.

The baby-sitter and I both noticed a plain black car parked down and across our tiny street. Two men were sitting in the car and I could feel them watching my house. I didn't have any idea what they thought they would find. I was just a mom and wife going through my life as best as I could. I wasn't frightened, I was irritated. Let 'em watch me – I had nothing to hide.

One Sunday morning I woke up to icy rain. The black car was across the street. It looked cold and dark. I took out a serving tray and a coffee carafe. I added two mugs, some cream and sugar and some fresh baked coffee cake onto the tray. Then I put on my warmest clothing and took the tray out to the car.

The hot coffee sent steamy clouds and the smell of rich, warm goodness into the air. I tapped on the window and it was immediately rolled down. I told them, if they were insisting on sitting out in the rain, that I might as well try to warm them up. A little while later the car was gone and the tray was sitting on my porch. The coffee and cake were gone and there was a note – "Thank you." I never saw the car again.

I heard nothing from Moe or Joe for almost a month. We were half-way through the deployment and I was looking forward to having my man back within my reach. We were on the countdown.

The next time Moe and Joe arrived at my house, they had an official looking document that said I needed to hand over the letters Mike had written during the deployment. They assured me they would be reviewed and returned promptly. I handed over the entire shoebox, as I mumbled that I hoped I didn't find out they were really just scam artists trying to get fodder for their next porn novels.

I made weekly phone calls to the numbers on the business cards they had left me. I always asked the same question – when would they be returning my letters? I didn't understand what the hold-up could be. The letters were never about the Navy or the submarine. They were about us and our family and our plans. In one letter, written shortly after the boat's departure, I told Mike I thought I might be pregnant. Then two more letters later, I told him I was not going to have a baby after all. His letter to me was sweet and encouraging. How could that possibly be a threat to our country's security?

My weekly phone calls turned into two and three times a week and sometimes twice a day. I was not just irritated anymore, I was flat out angry.

But, the good thing about the experience was that I was finding my spunk. In the past, I had always just succumbed to people in authority, especially men. I seldom stood up for myself. Moe and Joe made me furious and I came out of my timid fear of men to firmly plant my feet and say – "No more!"

I marched myself in the office of Naval Investigative Services and asked who the officer was who supervised Moe and Joe. I was told that person was not available. So I asked for the commander. Again, I was told he was not available. Next I asked for the director. I thought maybe I wasn't using the right words for "who is in charge here", so I kept trying. Each time I was told that person was not available. Finally, I said it's OK, I would wait. I settled in with my crocheting and made myself comfortable. When it got to be close to lunch time, I opened up my bag and pulled out my sandwich and chips. The sandwich was tuna with lots of onions – quite odoriferous. I read my book, wrote a letter to Mike and just waited.

It took about four hours before they realized I wasn't going anywhere and I was shown to a well-appointed office. The uniformed man behind the desk asked me what he could do for me. I told him I wanted my letters back. It was simple. If I did NOT have the letters back within 48 hours, I would have my attorney be in touch with them.

By the time I got home, Moe and Joe were at my house – with my box of letters. I signed a receipt and they left.

213

THIS PAGE INTENTIONALLY LEFT BLANK.

Gramma's Got a Gun

When I was in sixth grade my grandmother became very ill and could no longer live alone. My mother was pregnant with my younger brother but she welcomed my grandmother into our home agreeing to take care of the ailing woman whom she had grown to love as a mother.

I thought my grandmother was about the bravest woman I had ever known. I had listened to her stories of life on the farm in Texas and was fascinated at what I learned. I sat next to her and watched as she stitched homemade bonnets on her treadle sewing machine. She was resourceful and I admired how she made my mother stop the car so she could get out and pick the mustard greens along the highway. She wasted nothing and considered herself to be rich beyond measure.

By the time I reached eighth grade, one of my aunts rented a house down the street from us and moved Grandma in with her. Every weekend I went to Grandmas and stayed with her while my aunt went to the city to work in a beauty salon. Friday night through Monday morning, I was Grandmas constant companion. I didn't mind that I didn't get to be with my friends. I was doing what was important – I was caretaking my grandmother.

One Saturday evening, Grandma was hallucinating after being prescribed a new drug. She managed to use her walker and get herself to the living room. She whispered to me to hand her that gun while pointing to the broom. I had been warned that she could show signs of confusion and I went along with her request. She snatched the broom from me and pointed it toward the front door.

"You better git outta here!!" she screamed. "Git on down the road and leave usin's alone!! I've got a big ole shotgun here. I know how ta use it and I'll blow a hole rit thu ya!! Ya all just git off my porch!" She ranted on and on about getting off her porch and made me stand behind her as she continued in her protective mindset.

"Grandma, should I call the sheriff?" I asked – her response was – NO – she could handle this. I listened closely trying to share the sounds she was hearing, but I came up with nothing. After a while she calmed down and told me everything was OK. She asked me to help her get back to bed. Once she was settled back between her covers, I called my father and he came down to the house.

Grandma liked to sit on the porch and watch me sweep it clean each day when I was with her. I always encouraged her because I told her I could not sweep the porch unless she watched for places I was missing. We had the cleanest porch in town.

I called my father to come to the house after Grandma's shotgun episode; he asked me if I had sweep the porch that evening. I told him yes and he said Grandma must have heard whoever had dropped all those potato chips on the porch. Grandma was not hallucinating. There had definitely been someone on her front porch.

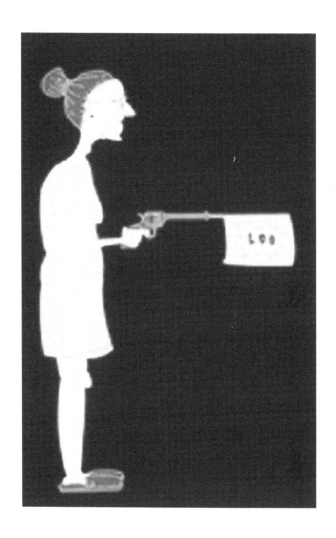

THIS PAGE INTENTIONALLY LEFT BLANK.

Scribble – Lee – Diddely -- Do

IT'S A TRICK

Thank you to Carolyn Peterson Bartee Hall for this reminder of her memory. Carolyn didn't know her way around Orange, San Bernardino or Riverside Counties, but she thought "How hard could it be? I have Map-Quested my route – so I'm good – Right?"

It's a trick. It's all a trick. Because if you don't already know the details of Southern California's freeway, highway, byway and/or driveway system dogma, i.e. codes, etc., you will be forever lost. The system creators, as well as helpful native residents, will smile upon you and with a very soothing, trust me, confident, purring voice, they'll direct you where to turn or there to turn, a numbered highway or a landmark to pass or some other simple direction. The signs will say North, South, East or West. The arrows will point left, right, up, down, sideways and it will all sound so easy and simple. But beware, they are not telling you everything. They are not telling you the one teeny, tiny piece of info that you must have to get from here to there. OH! That! Oops, too bad…

It's pretty much universal – no one really knows where they're going or exactly how to get where they think they want to go. But, know this, they are travelling fast, very fast, whether they actually arrive at the desired destination is immaterial as long as they move 80-120 mph. Going fast is the important thing and anyone travelling slower than anyone behind you is absolutely invisible.

If you're trying to merge to the left onto a freeway and a B16 long tanker is merging to the right from another freeway, which has divided 1/8th of a mile back, don't try to speed up. The tanker driver wants you gone. He does not want you ahead of him. The best thing to do is just ease on over into the bushes and pray for a quick death or evaporation. You don't have much of a choice because it seems that GOD is driving that truck. He is pissed and in no mood to save or bless any mere driver especially the slow ones. To top it all off, once you get away from that truck driving God, there is another one just ahead.

You may be armed with MapQuest and that's cool… well… sort of… If a friend or anyone offers you easy verbal directions NEVER hear them out. That too is a trick -- so don't do it. All those helpful people giving your "easy" directions are all from Milpitas, London and/or Outer Mongolia and have no more of an idea on how to get to the destination than you do.

You could ask the gas station attendant but there are none in sight. They are all behind the bulletproof, mirrored glass and are laughing their heads off at the directions they gave the last lost girls and boys. They might be taking bets on how long it will take for the confused drivers to return and ask them again for the same directions.

So maybe you could try the Circle K across the street. You get your pen; MapQuest maps; turn your car off (ooops the lights are still on so start the car and turn off the lights then turn the car back off); go into the store; ask the cashier if she could help you… She stares at you blankly. She says "I'm from Milpitas, but maybe Jose can help you. Hey! Jose! Tell this lady where to go!" Actually his name is Juan and after informing the cashier and you of that fact he says "Senora, how can I help you?" You tell him you need directions to Upland and he replies, "Oh Senora, go back that way. Go to 91, on 'bout ½ or fie/eits miles then get on 50N." You say "91?? East or West?" Juan says, "Mam… go East."

You take all Juan's directions and try to follow what he's told you and get on 91 East and after four or five minutes you never, EVER see a sign for 50N. That's when you think, "Shit! I was going

91 East in the first place and you must have gone too far. Maybe east is really west in Spanish, so you turn around again and look for 50N when you realize that you really DO speak Spanish and 50N means 15N!! Silly white girl!! I believe as soon as I find 15N, I'll be on my way home – maybe…

Sooner or later you're gonna see that you can get to 15N, but there are four to six directional signs hanging over the freeway exchanges each with an arrow. The cities are listed just above the arrows and you think – "Oh YEAH" until you realize every city is listed EXCEPT yours! OH NO! Where's Upland? There's no mention of Upland and you don't know what cities surround Upland.

Well… you do… kinda know where you want to go. You want to go to Upland. And I want to go on 15N but there are 4 exchanges for 15N so you get off on the one that says 91E and try to get help – AGAIN! Oh, I see, I'm in Riverside. I really didn't want to do this… but… I use the cell phone and call Linda for directions. It's after midnight and she has to be up by 5 a.m. to go to work. She answers the phone and stays on with me until I recognize where I am.

Hey!!! I know my way around LOST! BUT, to find FOUND you need to think slow, but drive faster than you think you should. Always know exactly where you want to go; get driving directions before you leave your house; and, no matter how awkward it feels, follow them to the letter. It may seem the long way around but it is probably the short way.

Linda and I prefer the mountains, but had to move to the "flatlands" because of her work. We talk of becoming FLATLANDERS. It's not something either of us aspired to. But having managed to leave my house, get lost in Corona, Riverside, San Bernardino on the 110, 215, 91, 15 and 60, I believe I may unwittingly become a flatlander.

I need a Calgon bath and hope it takes me away back to Northern California where everyone is equally lost.

GEOGRAPHICAL PULL

I've been spending a lot of time on our Bartee family history and I've dug up a lot of information about where our ancestors lived from their first arrival in the Americas. I'm beginning to believe that there is a geographical pull to places where our ancestors first planted roots. For example, I now live in an area where my ninth, tenth, and eleventh great grandfathers settled after their arrival into this country. In fact the local state park sits on the land that was once owed by one of those grandfathers.

During my search, I was connected with a woman from the Yarborough Organization who helped me piece together the answer to a family mystery. When I told her of the state park land, she forwarded to me several stories about connections to old family homesteads.

Thank you to Karen Mazock for these contributions:

******

I was talking to a researcher of another Yarbrough branch one day and telling her it didn't appear anyone was destined to find him. She was in her late 80s at the time, but she told me never to give up and related this story to me.

"I had been looking for my Alabama ancestor for a number of years and while I thought I'd narrowed his place of residence down, I was dismayed to find there were a number of men of about the same age with the same name in the area. This was in the days of snail mail where you would write for a document and, if you were lucky, you got a response from the court clerk in a month or so. I was on a small fixed income (social security) and rarely had extra money to order documents, especially when they may not even be the records I needed. So, I save my money and my kids and grandkids helped by giving me cash presents for birthdays, mother's day and Christmas.

Even with their help, I could only afford to go by bus and spend one night there.

"I can't tell you how excited I was. I rode all night on the bus, hoping to be at the courthouse when it opened and spend the entire day there. I had planned to spend the night there and my bus back home left early the next morning. The best laid plans ... The first thing that happened was the main road was temporarily closed due to spring flooding -- the water was over the bridge. We were delayed until nearly sunrise, so I got to the courthouse much later in the day than I'd planned.

"I told the clerk what I was looking for and she took to a room in the basement - 'the archives' she called it. She opened the door, turned on the light and left. When I went in, I was so disappointed I sank to the floor and tears flowed. It was a room of shelves, and each shelf was piled with loose papers -- wills, estate papers, etc. There was no organization or indexing at all. It would have taken a good month to look through those papers, and I had only a couple of hours.

As I sat on the floor, my face streaked with tears and my heart filled with disappointment.. A piece of paper fell from a shelf. I picked it up to replace and, at that moment, I came the closest to having a heart attack that I will ever come without actually having one. In my hand was the Will of William Yarbrough -- and it was my William! I looked at the stack of papers from where the will had fallen and there was the entire estate file. So, never give up -- sometimes you get help from very unexpected places."

My naval husband was transferred to Virginia and I spent every spare moment in graveyards, state archives and courthouses. I managed to link my line to Richard Yarborough (the immigrant) and, using a bunch of old land surveys, I managed to locate Richard's Virginia property. Amazingly enough, the landmarks and boundaries really hadn't changed that much over the years (referring to the meanderings of the Mattaponi River. Once I was sure I had found his property, I started looking for a road to a farmhouse. I was all set to ask the present owner if they knew of any graves on the property since no one seems to know where Richard's wife was buried.

I was so disappointed to see multiple No Trespassing signs and the gate to the road was chained and padlocked. But, thinks I, surely there would be no harm if I just slipped over the fence to stand on the property for a moment. Strangely, when I stepped on the property, a feeling of belonging settled over me. I can't explain it better than that. It was the most peaceful feeling -- until my revelry was suddenly disturbed by the sound of deep, angry barking and running toward me, teeth bared, were the two biggest Rottweiler's I've ever seen. They seemed to have no understanding at all of my peaceful co-mingling with the land. Believe it or not, I ran to the fence I had climbed and cleared it with a single bound.

In 1892, my grandmother's family migrated from Keysport, Illinois to Indian Territory. She was 4 years old. She had no memory of crossing the Mississippi, and figured maybe she was asleep at the time.

She remembered stopping at night. Her mom and dad slept on the ground and she and her brother slept in the wagon. Along the side of the wagon were feed troughs where her dad put grain for the horses. To this day I can see her leaning closer to me and saying softly, "And you know, Karen, sometimes very late at night when it is very quiet, I fancy I can still hear those horses munching." And I heard them, too.

They had their old blue hound dog with them (the children's pet). One morning the father had hitched up the horses and headed out, not realizing the dog was asleep under the wagon. The wheel ran over him and killed him. My grandmother said she and her brother cried for days. Her father was a minister, so he took the time to dig a grave and bury the dog and gave him a Christian burial. Grandma always cried when she related that part of the trip.

They didn't stay in Indian Territory long. Very shortly after their arrival, Indians swooped down upon their cabin, tomahawks in hand. Grandma could describe vividly the war paint on their faces, colors and designs. She said they didn't do much other than make a lot of noise and raise a lot of dust. But that was enough for my great grandmother. She told her husband, "That's it, we are returning to civilization!" They traveled back and settled in Lebanon, Missouri. This always tickled me as at that time, Lebanon had less than 2,000 people in the entire area.

GOING HOME

I grew up in a small town in the agricultural bread basket of California during a time when everything was changing. The people I grew up with were born in a time of straight-laced values of the 50s and by the time we finished college, we experienced the age of anything goes of the 60s. We were faced with hard choices and tests on our value systems.

Small town life isn't for everyone. I believed, at age 18, that it was not the life for me. I cried through my graduation ceremony, but my tears were generated from happiness. I was happy that I would be leaving Brentwood, and everything about it, for a life in a bigger city. I wasn't sure where I was going, but I knew it was away from where I was.

Every time I returned to Brentwood to be with my parents, I was quiet about my presence. I didn't attempt to find old friends. I simply would lay low until it was time for me to go. I had no desire to become a member of the community.

Now... I would love to be able to go back to Brentwood. But I would not want to return to today's Brentwood with its sprawling subdivisions, homeowner associations, shopping centers and multi-lane boulevards. I long for the town where the salesman at the auto dealership tells the kids to hurry along to school and knows them each by name AND their parents phone number. There's something comforting to live in a place where a big crime is big news because it happens so seldom. It would be nice to be able to re-connect with old schoolmates, but I'm not sure how many of them actually remained or returned to Brentwood.

When I go on Facebook and see the old photos of my hometown, I get nostalgic. I want to climb inside a time machine and go back. Sometimes I want a "do over." It's like, if I knew then what I know now… well we know how that goes don't we?

I choose a sailor as my life partner. I did that knowing that I would not be putting down any real roots as I had experienced growing up. It is not surprising to me that I sometimes want to be back in my childhood place and time. On the other hand, I'm a realist. I make a home out of where my head lies at night. That's the way it is. That's the way it must be.

It is ironic that I now live in the country, in a very small town, where my ninth, tenth and eleventh great-grandparents from the 1600's called home. It just so happens that the house we live in may be on ground that my grandparents may have owned. I did this by accident and not design. So maybe we really can go home again even if we do it unconsciously.

MORE, MORE, MORE

I was writing little stories and posting them on Facebook or on my blog, *Immortal Alcoholic*, but I was always being asked for more and more and more.

Every time I would write a story, it would remind me of another instance, memory, adventure or something else. Someone said – *"Linda write a book of your short stories. That way they are available for everyone to read when they want to read them."*

OK. Here they are. It was a bit of a trial to decide when to stop because I have a very good memory about some things. I just didn't know if I should keep going until I felt my memory banks were empty or if I should pick a place and turn off the computer.

While the majority of this book is about childhood memories and my home town, it is also about other parts of my life. It's funny how a childhood memory will spark an adult memory.

There is a vague theme to the stories – a direction so to speak. In the end it is about going home. It's about being at home. It's about appreciating "home."

And home encompasses people from home whether it be family or friends. This book is not a life story. It's a book of memories. Some may be exact, others may not be as anyone else remembers it.

I have several other writing projects on my plate, but I hope to write another short story book in the not-to-far-distant future

I hope you have enjoyed what's between these pages. I also hope you have been inspired to write your own book of memory reminders.

ABOUT THE AUTHOR

Linda Bartee Doyne grew up in Contra Costa County's Brentwood, California during a time without cell phones. She is from the generation that used streetlights as the alarm to go home. She drank from the water hose and rode in the back of an open pick-up truck. She knew that if she misbehaved, her actions could and often were relayed back to her parents in what seemed like light-speed communication.

Linda is the author of "The Immortal Alcoholic's Wife" (available on Amazon.com) and a "Workbook for Caretakers of End-Stage Alcoholics" (available only on her blog, Immortal Alcoholic on blogspot.com). Besides her blog she is the founder and operator of three support groups for the family and friends of alcoholics.

Upcoming in late spring 2016 a major cable network documentary film on alcoholism will be premiered. Linda has been a major contributor in the production of this film. Also scheduled for late spring or early summer 2016 is the sequel to The Immortal Alcoholic's Wife which will focus on her husband's journey through alcoholism. A Bartee Family History book is also being researched and written.

THIS PAGE INTENTIONALLY LEFT BLANK

Take all the notes and things you've written on these blank pages and turn it into your own book of memories that were sparked by the reminders of memories in this book.

I can't wait to read it!

Made in the USA
Charleston, SC
14 August 2015